The Rhoades family (back) Mom Ruby, Jan, Jeanne, Dad Benton (front) Becca and Bobby.

LLANO GRANDE

Growing Up as a Missionary Child in Ecuador

*To Joan,
Live the adventure!
Jeanne*

Jeanne M. Rhoades Smucker

Hawthorne Publishing

Copyright © 2015 Jeanne M. Rhoades Smucker

ISBN: 978-0-9963949-0-1

All rights reserved

No part of this book may be reproduced or utilized in any form or by any means, electronic or mechanical, including photocopying and recording, or by any information storage and retrieval system, without permission in writing from the publisher.

Hawthorne Publishing
15601 Oak Road
Carmel, IN 46033
317-867-5183

www.hawthornepub.com

DEDICATION

In loving memory of my parents

J. Benton and Ruby Frantz Rhoades,

my husband Mark and my son Mike

and

For my children

Bethany, Rachel and Jabar

who remember climbing in the corncribs where their father used to play.

I hope that they can now also picture where their mother played.

ACKNOWLEDGMENTS

This book would not have been possible without the coming together of two families—the Tasiguano-Guaman family and my own Rhoades family. Mercedes Tasiguano, Enrique Tasiguano and Andrés Guaman all took the time from their busy lives to share their memories and their rich heritage with me. Elizabeth Guaman and her husband Fabian Quishpe generously opened their home to me and made it a comfortable base from which to reconnect with Llano Grande. They have now become a second family to me.

To my siblings—Janet Rhoades, Becca Choitz and Bob Rhoades: thank you for listening to some of these stories. You remembered details that make this a richer narrative.

The Church of the Brethren generously opened its archives for me to read correspondence between my parents and the mission board. Especially, appreciation is due to the archivist Bill Kostlevy, who gathered the files I needed as well as recommending lodging and meals while I was in Elgin, Illinois. The archived back issues of the *Gospel Messenger* provided background information that in my youth I would not have known or appreciated. My mother collected old photographs in a cardboard box that I brought home with me. I'm not sure who gets the credit for taking the pictures, but I am grateful for the many memories that the pictures brought back for me.

Thank you to Lyn Jones, whose workshop on memoir writing at the Indiana Writers' Center got me started and taught me much about making a story come alive. Thank you to Nancy Baxter and Hawthorne Publishing for helping to craft the stories into one coherent book.

INTRODUCTION

Third Culture Kid

I didn't know what the term "third culture kid" meant when I was growing up, but I did know the feeling. When my graduate school classmates responded to the picture of my family of origin, I was overwhelmed with the same intense feelings of shame that I knew too well from my adolescence.

I was in my mid-forties, with children in junior high school, studying for a PhD in nursing. Since my interest was families, I had signed up for a course on family systems and we were to bring a picture of our family of origin. Sorting through old photographs I settled on one of my family when I was in second grade. My dad sits on the right in a grey three-piece-suit and a dark tie. His hair is combed back in a neat pompadour; his face in a relaxed, open smile. Next to him, I stand with a face so like his, though more serious. My blond hair is pulled back in two pony-tails, and Jan, in first grade, is next to me in a matching grey striped dress with a red collar. Her equally blond hair is in a page-boy with straight bangs. Bobby, who has just turned two, sits between us, wearing a tweed collarless jacket; his long, white shirt collars reach almost to his shoulders. He looks straight ahead with a somewhat puzzled look. Sitting beside him is Mom in a navy nylon seersucker dress; her curly brown hair is brushed away from her face and she smiles at the camera. And leaning on her knee is Becca, three years old, her blond head tilted sweetly at the photographer. Her slender hand rests in Mom's and the light pink flower girl dress hangs from her slender, little body. This photo became the frontispiece for this book and I believe it reveals a good deal about each individual in it.

I wanted to share the picture for my class because it was taken shortly after Becca had surgery for cancer and we were all together again. In the process of explaining that to the class, however, I had to mention that we lived in Ecuador at the time. Suddenly the focus was not on the family crisis I had hoped to share. Instead, eyes turned toward me and the professor commented, "Ecuador! How interesting to grow up in another country!" My cheeks burned, my heart pounded, my mouth went dry, tears stung my eyes and my chin quivered. I had no words to respond, and the professor noted my distress and quickly moved on to the next student.

I was left wondering about my intense reaction. In my mind I suddenly found myself back in eighth grade, just returned from Ecuador, at a church conference. Around lunch with other missionary kids, we happily talked about memories of our childhoods. Then a boy my age, who had himself grown up in India, turned to me and said, "Ecuador, Ecuador, Ecuador! All you ever talk about is Ecuador. Do you think it is such a big deal that you grew up in Ecuador?"

At that earlier time also, my cheeks had burned with shame as I fought back tears. From then on when others shared stories of their childhoods, I usually just listened, remembering my own stories but ashamed to share them. So, now, with children the same age as I had been when this comment was made and sitting in a classroom, I finally began to face the turmoil without a name.

The intensity of my reaction that day in class still puzzles me, but I find it repeated in the stories of other children who grew up as I did, between two cultures. One such child, who grew up in half a dozen countries in the Middle East and Europe, described her experience on return to the States this way: "No one knew, or cared, about what I knew, and I didn't know what everyone else knew. Same age, same language, same accent, same neighborhood; worlds apart in experience." I had spent a lifetime trying to bridge the gap, to be able to relate to my peers on the same terms. Now, in graduate school years after my childhood, it seemed I had blown my cover, quite by accident.

It wasn't until a few years later that I learned that there actually was a name and considerable research was being done on us children who had grown up as I had. I was at another church conference where a young man eagerly told the group about his plans to go with his family to a mission in Africa. "We've told our children how exciting it will be to be able to come home and tell their friends about seeing giraffes and elephants walking by the window," he said.

"And, their friends couldn't care less, " I replied frankly. "All they will care about is whether your kids dress right and know the current music and jokes."

"I know, I know" he said. "I have read all about third culture kids." That was the first time I knew that we actually had a name and that there were volumes written about how children like me had struggled with identity.

We balk at the question, "Where are you from?" Where, indeed? People usually ask the question to try to place you, to try to understand what makes you who you are. Saying "Ecuador" brings the conversation to a halt. The person asking has no way to relate. While in Ecuador I was always aware that I was a guest, a foreigner, so I really can't say that I am from Ecuador. But, then, where am I from?

Having become a Mennonite as an adult, I became familiar with people "playing the Mennonite game." That means responding to where someone says they are from with things like: "Troyer, from Harrisonburg... I have family there. Do you know...?" Or "Yoder from Goshen ... I grew up in Elkhart." After marrying a Mennonite farm boy from Ohio, I took on his heritage as my own. I became the daughter-in-law who at Christmas made anise cookies from the recipe that my mother-in-law's great grandmother brought from Switzerland. The blue Currier and Ives dishes that once served five growing farm boys now sit on my suburban kitchen shelves. I quickly learned to answer the question of where I was from with, "My husband is from Wayne County, Ohio." People could "play the Mennonite game" forever on Smucker from Wayne County and I never had to deal with the awkward silence following "I grew up in Ecuador." And, anyway, am I really from there when I am clearly not Ecuadorian?

In 1972, when I was preparing for my wedding, my father stopped in Indianapolis on his way to somewhere. He was still always going somewhere. I drove out to the airport to have lunch with him during his lay-over. Being at the airport was always an exhilarating experience for me—people with suitcases hurrying to their flights, the adventure of what lay ahead. Since there were no security gates separating travelers from visitors, we enjoyed a light lunch at one of the restaurants that served as destinations for people who came to the airport to watch planes coming and going. Then I hugged Dad and watched him head to the boarding gate.

As I drove back to the apartment that I shared with two other single women, I suddenly was struck by the fact that, with marriage, I was finally "hanging up" my passport. After returning from Ecuador when I was in eighth grade, I had continued to yearn to travel. One year while I was in college, I spent a summer in Puerto Rico. Then, after graduation, I went to Brazil for two years to test out my own calling to mission. But no more of that now. Now I would marry and stay put. All was changing.

After returning from Brazil, I had begun to imagine a career in international health care. First, though, I needed to get a master's degree in public health. That is when Mark came into my life, and with Mark came roots. With the image of hanging up my passport came another image of being at a crossroad. The truth is that I had less idea of what lay down the road of marriage than I had of what international work would entail. So, though it did not involve travel, I was again embarking on an adventure into the unknown. That is a story is for another time.

Although the graduate class brought my dilemma into stark focus for me, I know that each of my siblings felt our difference in their own way. Becca noticed it when she was only three years old. She looked out of the hospital window at children playing in the snow and asked Mom, "What language are they playing in?" When Mom told her it was English, she immediately stopped speaking Spanish until she returned to Ecuador. Then she was dismayed not to be able on her return to tell her little Ecuadorian friends about her new doll; she had forgotten Spanish. Jan remembers a classmate in college asking her, "Why don't you ever talk about your childhood? Did something terrible happen?" Like so many third culture kids, we found it was easier to talk about our childhoods with a 95-year-old former missionary kid in our parents' retirement community than with our age mates who had never left this country.

One of the hardest parts of making our home in a country different from our parents' passport country is figuring out how to fit in when we came "home" (our parents' home) on furlough. Grandparents and aunts and uncles I didn't remember grasped at me as I shivered on airport tarmacs. They thrust a warm coat, which used to belong to someone else, onto me. Someone actually gave us used, out-of-style clothing once with the comment, "You can wear it. It doesn't matter on the mission field."

Attending a school for missionaries' children gave me the false sense that I knew how to be "American." I did not. Before furloughs, we scanned American magazines to figure out what was in fashion and had a seamstress make us the outfit we would wear on the plane. I remember hearing of one missionary family returning from Africa who had carefully dressed to "not stand out." Yet, the parents noticed as they walked through the airport, that people turned and stared at their family. When the parents looked around, they found their children walking along with their suitcases balanced on their heads!

I feel like I am finally reaching the point of being able to openly talk about growing up in Ecuador. I volunteer in a free clinic where I do much of my work in Spanish, and people often comment on my fluency and my native accent. With recent immigrants from Latin America, my childhood does not seem exotic. It just gives me a connection.

When I spoke at my father's memorial service, I acknowledged the incredible gift my parents gave us of a childhood in Ecuador. And I am grateful for that gift—a secure sense of family, the ease of moving among cultures, fluency in Spanish that has served each of us in our various fields of work. Nothing could ever replace that.

It has taken returning to Ecuador, more than 55 years after leaving, and reconnecting with my close childhood friend Mercedes to bring me to the place of putting down in writing memories of my experiences growing up. While I am there, Mercedes' brother Enrique asks, "What project brings you here at this time?" Do foreigners always have to have a project to come to Ecuador?

I reply, "I came looking for that part of me that I left behind when I left this community as a child."

"And, what have you found?" he asks. I smile. I am still working on that.

I know that each "third culture kid" has his or her unique experience. Yet we all have struggled to figure out how to integrate what others view as an exotic and unusual childhood with what to us was the only childhood we knew. But, then, isn't every childhood unique and any memoir reflective of that uniqueness?

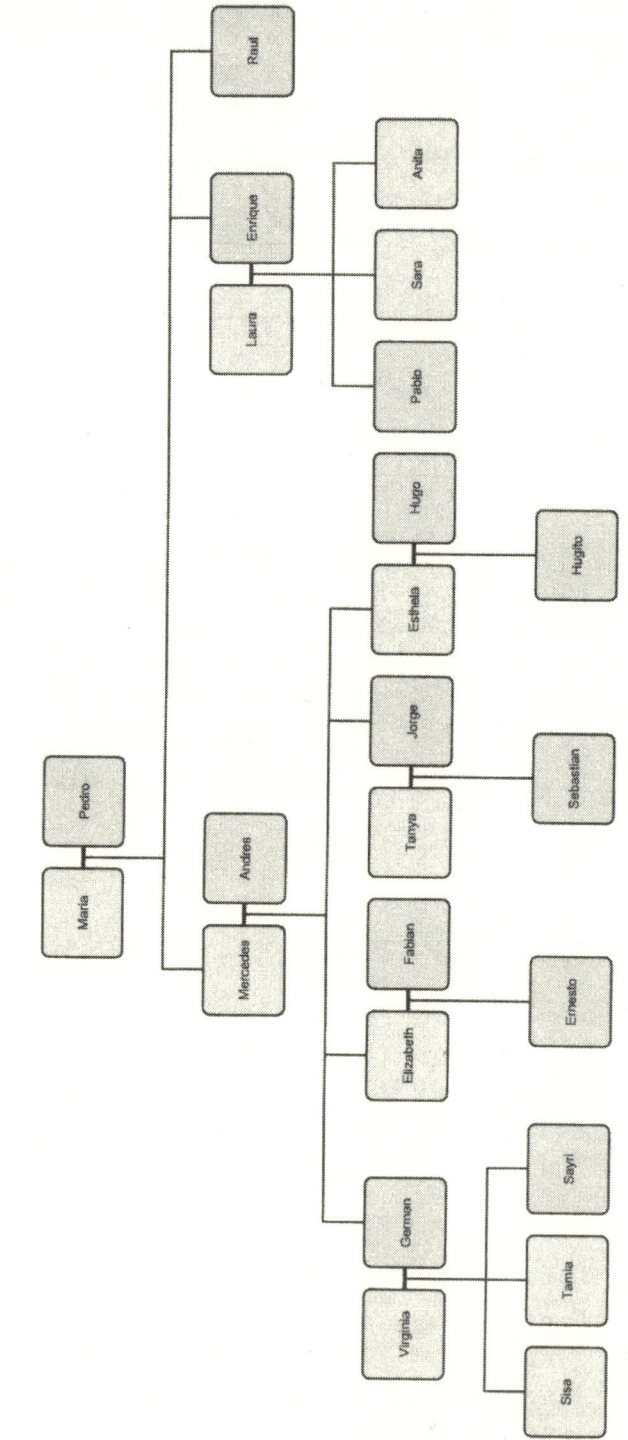

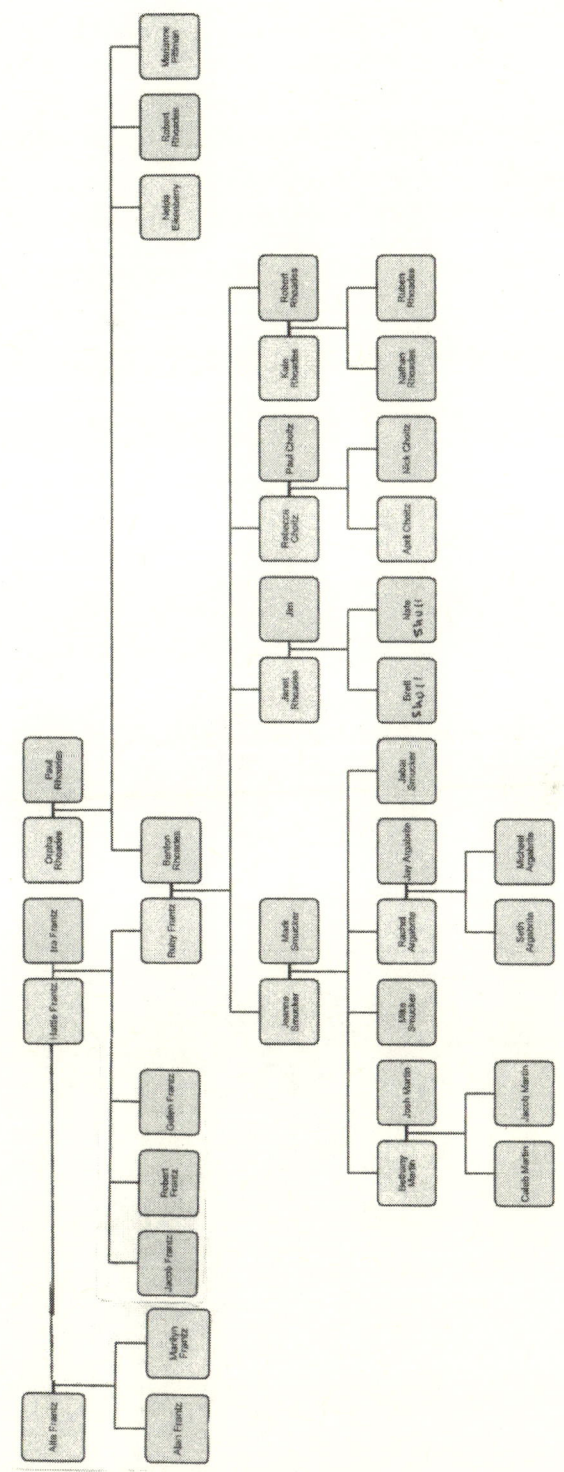

xiii

1
Llano Grande

It is 2014 and I am on a climate-controlled tour bus filled with Purdue University undergraduate students heading north out of Quito, Ecuador. It is the final day of the medical brigade with Timmy Global Health, a not-for-profit working to expand worldwide health care, and the students are looking forward to a break from the week of hard work providing medical care to the people in the slums of South Quito. They will be visiting the equator and doing some souvenir shopping in the artisan market of Otovalo.

I am not going where they are going. Instead, I'm on my way home, home to the place I spent my childhood as a missionary's kid, home to the place I left over fifty-five years ago, home, I hope, to find the child I left behind when I returned to the States at the age of fourteen.

I had hoped to make this trip with my husband several years ago. Those plans were interrupted when he was diagnosed with leukemia. Six months after his death, our son was diagnosed with terminal cancer and I had to retire abruptly to care for him, and travel plans were put on hold. Less than a week after my son died, I got an email from Timmy Global Health saying that it desperately needed a nurse for its upcoming brigade to Quito, Ecuador. Would I consider joining them? "Is it too soon?" I asked my daughters.

"What do you mean, 'too soon'? It is just the right time," they responded. My friends agreed with them.

On that first trip with Timmy Global Health, I had spent a day and a half in Llano Grande, reconnecting with my childhood friend Mercedes and getting to know her family. Her adult daughter Elizabeth had told me that the next time I came, I was to stay longer and in her home. So, here I am, 2,795 miles from my hometown of Indianapolis, on that "next time," finally coming home. I will be staying for ten days in Llano Grande with Elizabeth and her family, visiting with my friends. I feel a mixture of excitement and apprehension because I hardly know these people.

Earlier in the week, I had talked the bus driver into dropping me off in Llano Grande when he was taking the students to the equator. At first, he hesitated, but when I told him that I was going home to where I spent my childhood, he actually altered his route to be able to drop me off. The Pan-American Highway that used to be cobblestone is now a four-lane highway.

This morning, the bus stops at the second entrance to Llano Grande, a road named for Calixto Muzo, one of the first indigenous leaders who spoke up for the rights of the native people of Llano Grande. The bus driver is concerned because no one is there to meet me. I call Mercedes on her cell phone and assure the driver that she is on her way, so it is okay to leave me here.

I wait with my suitcase by the highway while loaded semis roar past, blowing dust in my face. A group of students gathers on the far corner, book bags over their shoulders, cell phones to their ears. Young mothers hurry by carrying loaded grocery bags and clutching the hands of little children, and a stray dog sniffs along the curb.

The whole scene could be set in any metropolitan area in Latin America. Nothing looks like what I remember. Trying to remain calm, I wonder if I even belong here, or ever did. Then, I see Mercedes coming up the street, and I know this is the place where I am supposed to be. She has hired a pickup truck through the informal taxi system of Llano Grande. The driver tosses my suitcase into the back of the truck, and we climb into the cab. A short drive takes us to Elizabeth's house.

2
Humitas and Rhubarb Pie

After we arrive at Elizabeth's house, I unload my luggage in the guest room. Then Mercedes gets out a little notebook in which she has written a tentative itinerary for my visit. "Is there anything else you want to do during the ten days you will be here?" she asks. She knows that I want to revisit my life as a child in Llano Grande and hope to recall and learn more about the traditions I was only vaguely aware of then as well as about the Ecuador of today.

I'm sure I will think of other things later. But first, something that is homey and simple. "I want you to show me how to make humitas," I say. How well I remember being invited to local homes on special days and being served *humitas*, the Ecuadorian version of tamales. I loved to unwrap them from the cornhusks that left their imprint on the steamed corn cake inside. I have tried to make them at home, but the corn in the States is not the same as we had in Ecuador.

"The timing is perfect," Mercedes says. "The corn is just getting ripe enough for humitas. We have time to do this before lunch."

Elizabeth drives us in their pickup truck to a field at the far end of the village. Mercedes's childhood home once stood on this property. Now only the field remains. As I walk among the cornstalks, learning how to recognize the ears that are ripe, I am overwhelmed with gratitude for the fact that I am here and that I have the privilege to step into this world. At the far end of the field, there is a guava tree, and almost as if it were waiting for me, it has one guava on it. I stand there in the cornfield breaking open the pod, with the black seeds covered by a fuzzy, white pulp that I suck off.

After we have picked a big bag of corn, Mercedes asks me if I remember *chupando caña*, sucking on cane. Of course I do. She cuts one of the stalks of corn, peels it with her teeth and then offers it to me. We stand there in the field, chewing the stalk until it is dry and spitting the pulp on the ground.

Mercedes's eight-year-old grandson Ernesto brings ears of corn to her to check whether they are ripe enough. Then he starts jumping out from behind stalks to try to spook her. When we get back to the truck, Mercedes is nowhere to be found. Little Ernesto says, "*Yo me encargo de la busca*. I will take charge of the search," and jumps up on the wall to go looking for his grandmother. He finds her still among the rows of corn.

"Could you also teach us to make pie?" Mercedes asks as we drive back from the cornfield to Elizabeth's house. "There is one place in Otovalo that says they sell pie, but it is not like the missionaries used to make." That seems like a fair exchange to me. I learn to make humitas and I teach them to make pie.

After lunch the whole family gathers around the table for a *minga* of corn-shelling. Even Mercedes's husband Andrés and Elizabeth's husband Fabian join in the work. Mingas were a regular part of life in the community of Llano Grande when I was growing up, dating back to the Incas. The term refers to community work or work among friends when they need help from each other. In addition to this, mingas usually include a feast to celebrate the hard work and collaboration. The mission school hosted as many as six mingas in one year, getting the school buildings restored, the grounds cleared, and the road maintained.

The corn kernels are large and firm enough to shell from the cobs by hand. We grind them in an electric grinder, though it was once done on a stone, then we go out looking for eggs. The chickens are free range, but a neighbor girl shows us where she found two nests, one under some shrubs and the other under the concrete washboard. We take all but one egg from each of the two nests we find, leaving one egg so that the chickens will keep laying.

While we are working on the humitas, Mercedes tells me about her mother making a hundred humitas in one day and taking them into Quito to sell. Her mother would leave before sunrise, a basket of humitas slung from a head strap into her back. Mercedes's father

Pedro was already working in the city for the whole week. When the children woke up, they would walk to where the bus picked up passengers from Llano Grande, Mercedes carrying her little brother Raul and holding Enrique's hand. They would look in the dust for the tire tracks of the bus to see if their mother was already gone. When they saw she was gone, they would return home and fall back asleep. When they awoke again, Mercedes and Enrique would hurry to school, where they would get breakfast and lunch. Little Raul stayed at home alone. There was no food in the house, and it broke her heart when she was with him and he would pull on her skirt and say, "Ñaña, sister, I'm hungry." Raul started first grade when he was four so he could get the breakfast and lunch at school.

At one point, that ninety-one-year-old mother Tia Maria motions to me to come and sit with her in the living room. She has come to join in the family's welcome of me. "*Hermanita.* Little sister," she says, holding my hand in hers and looking into my eyes. "Hermanita." I present her with a copy of a picture of her late husband Pedro that I found among my father's things. Pedro sits in his red striped poncho, eyes closed, his harp resting against his shoulder. The bow of the harp has the brightly painted head of a Native American carved into it. His fingers pluck the strings.

Tia Maria talks about how many years she and Pedro were married. "We had such happy times. He played his harp and sang to me." I recall him well and find myself asking about his death. She says, "He was supposed to play the harp at an event. Someone was coming to pick him up. Instead, they mugged him and stole his harp. What was he to do without his harp?" After that he was so sad and depressed, she tells me, that he drank himself to death. "But, oh, how beautifully he played and sang."

Elizabeth gets out pictures of her grandfather's funeral. "We had just gotten back from Spain. By then, he was drinking a lot. He went to the *chicharia* to drink and fell down on the floor. No one bothered to check on him. They just covered him up with his poncho. By the time we got there, he was almost dead. At the hospital, they said there was no hope." The pictures show a flower-draped casket being carried through the community. A small boy in a red poncho walks in front, ringing a large brass bell. In spite of his many years of alcoholism and unfaithfulness to his wife and family,

Pedro was clearly still respected enough that the whole community came out to bid farewell to him, the harpist of Llano Grande. "But, oh, how beautifully he played and sang."

When it is time to assemble the humitas, Tia Maria joins us in the kitchen. "It's hard to believe that I used to make one hundred humitas in one day to sell in Quito, grinding the corn between stones and steaming the humitas in a pot over an open fire," she says as she expertly spoons the thin corn and egg mixture into the green corn husks and adds fresh white cheese or raisins. Then she folds the husks snuggly around dough and places the humitas into a pot to steam. Even now, Tia Maria still makes foods to sell to passers-by from a little table on her front porch.

Late in the afternoon, we get to work on the rhubarb pie. They tell me that the word "pie" in native Kichwa means "thank you," in respect to food. Or, perhaps it is short for Spanish "*Dios se lo pague*," or "May God repay you," the local way of saying "Thank you." Elizabeth's husband Fabian has a notebook, writing down what I am doing and recording any hints. He seems to be the cook in the family. I am working from what I can remember of my mother-in-law's recipe, using fruit from a large stand of rhubarb behind Mercedes's house. I don't remember the native people eating rhubarb when I was small, so I ask her where it came from.

"We got starts from Señora Ruby's garden. Do you remember?" My mother. Of course I remember the rhubarb growing in the garden outside the wall in front of our house. The temperate climate must have been ideal for growing rhubarb because the leaves were huge, large enough for us to hide under when we played hide-and-seek after dusk, or perhaps the leaves just seemed huge because we were small.

A letter from my mother to the folks in Indiana and Illinois makes a comment or two on the situation of both rhubarb and the need for reassuring faraway loved ones:

July 6, 1952
Dear folks,
Though it's Benton's turn to write, I'll at least start off this time. Francisco asked off for two days, his wife's parents came and they are taking a little trip north of here. So Benton is doing chores, morning and

night. The other reason I wanted to write was to tell Dad Rhoades that yesterday I baked a rhubarb pie. I wasn't sure Benton would consider that an item of information but I just wanted you to know that your son didn't get so badly stuck on a wife after all…
Ruby

This afternoon, as I'm creating the old favorite pie, we are using rendered pork fat as lard, and it is soft and runny, so the dough is kind of "short" but workable. But putting it into a square pan is challenging. They have one round pie plate, but the second pie goes into a square pan. We chop up the rhubarb and I make the filling with sugar, flour, and eggs, noting that the free-range eggs have yolks that are so yellow they are almost orange.

For the brown sugar in the topping, we need to grate *raspadura*, a dark loaf of raw sugar. I remember my mother bringing raspadura home from the market. The large chunks of sugar had a rich molasses smell. While Mom grated it for brown sugar, we begged for pieces to suck on. Now I mix the grated brown sugar with flour and butter and spread it over the rhubarb. The pies are a hit. Ernesto even comes to me later and asks if he can have another piece. We are saving some for his uncle Enrique, but I help him sneak a sliver for himself.

I have heard that the memory of tastes endures longer than any other memory, and I am certainly lost in memories as I savor the warm humitas and the chunks of raspadura.

Chapter 3
Births and Traditions

Although our family straddled two cultures, North American and Ecuadorian, I am aware how much we owe to the Midwest. Still today, midwestern roots run deep in my family. My father came from a small farming community in western Illinois, and my mother was from a college town in northern Indiana. They met and were married in that same college town, and I was born while they were in seminary in Chicago. That was also where they made plans to go to Ecuador as missionaries.

Our odyssey began right after World War II. I was born at Bethany Hospital in Chicago the year the war ended. According to my mother, at that time Dad was taking a seminary course on making hospital visits. So, he was trying out what he was learning on Mom. Meanwhile, Mom was "dancing" around the bed in her hospital gown, singing Johnny Mercer's then-popular song, "You have to accentuate the positive, eliminate the negative; latch on to the affirmative. Don't mess with Mr. In-Between." I'm hoping that she did not mean that I was the negative she wanted to eliminate, but I'm sure she just wanted to get things moving.

Jan was born at home, soon after we arrived in Ecuador. I don't remember it either, but I have heard the stories. Mom had boiled bed linens and hung them in a bag over the bathtub. I suppose that was thought to sterilize them. They had had guests for a chili dinner, so when Mom went into labor, she thought it might be indigestion from the chili. The arrangements were for a doctor and nurse to come to the house. I assume the doctor was Dr. Ovalle, a Columbian doctor with close ties to the American embassy and, as we learned later, the CIA. He would continue to advise the missionaries on medical matters until the Mission Board sent a doctor to join the mission. I remember the name of the nurse was Mrs. Donsiger, a prim German immigrant. Unfortunately, she and the doctor had had a disagreement and were not on speaking terms, so when one was in the room, the other would leave. I'm guessing that Dad was there for this birth though not for mine. After the baby was born, they called me into the room. I was eighteen months old, but they put the baby on my lap and let me hold her. Mom says I never showed sibling rivalry, perhaps because I was there from the start and Jan never took my mother away from me.

The later siblings Becca and Bob were born at the Clinica Ayora. It was built like a typical Spanish-style home around an open courtyard, with all the rooms opening onto the courtyard. The delivery room and the nursery were at one end of the portico, and there were chairs on the porch outside the consultation rooms for women to wait for office visits. The patient rooms were along the other sides of the patio. I do remember going to look at the babies in the nursery. Bobby was remarkable for his thick curls. I also remember that the nurse who answered call bells sat at a table on the porch, making sanitary napkins with cotton batting (or was it kapok?) and gauze.

The new mothers had to stay in bed for five days, so they were weak when they got up. I felt so grown up when my mother asked me to help her walk around the patio when she was finally allowed up. Across the street from the maternity hospital was a public park. It had a tower with a walkway spiraling around it that we loved to climb up and run down. There was also a small lake with paddleboats that we would beg to ride.

On my return to Ecuador and before I arrived in Llano Grande, I struggled to recognize any landmarks in the modern, bustling city of Quito. With the college students in the medical brigade, I had ridden the tour bus through wide, paved streets, jammed with noisy cars. Only the tour of the "Old City" took me to familiar places like the Plaza San Francisco, where Mom shopped for produce, or the Plaza de Independencia with its imposing government buildings. Then our tour bus passed the park I remembered from the times

Becca and Bob were born. The tower and lake with paddleboats were still there. When I recognized the park, I glanced up, and there was a large, modern maternity hospital with the name Hospital Maternidad Clinica Ayora. The same hospital, yet not the same.

Mom said that Becca was kind of a homely baby. Dad, though, told her that she was beautiful. Her head was misshapen from the long labor and she had some bruising or broken blood vessels in her eyes. Sometime during her infancy, Mom and Dad left her with me while they went to church because I was not feeling well. I had strict orders not to get her out of the crib. I was five years old. She started crying and I saw that her diaper was wet, so I got her out and put her on the Bathinette. I'm not sure how I did that, but I do remember changing the diaper, especially since it was fastened with diaper pins. As I was finishing, Mom and Dad walked in. After reprimanding me for getting Becca out of her crib, Dad laughed. "You made the diaper loose enough to fit me."

After having three girls, my parents were excited when Bob was born to finally have a boy. Dad had been to a coastal town where he bought a crate of plums, which sat in the middle of the kitchen floor. Before Mom had a chance to can the plums, she went into labor, so Dad and Maria, the young local girl who helped in our house, were left to do it, though neither one knew a lot about canning. In spite of the kitchen floor being sticky from the broken jars and spilled juice, there was soon something lovely: a row of sparkling jars of canned plums lining a shelf in the basement. I have always loved home-canned plums. I remembered this scene many years later, when my grandson Caleb helped me pick up and can plums while his mother was in the hospital giving birth to his baby brother Jacob.

Mom had also asked Maria to let the hems out of some of Becca's dresses. Imagine her embarrassment when Dad brought Becca to visit in dresses to her ankles! Generous hems allowed us to get the most wear out of our clothing, but they were not meant to be let out all at once.

Dad's story about Bob's birth included a long labor. Dad was in the delivery room, and the doctor said, "You have three daughters, right?" When Dad agreed, the doctor lifted Bob by the feet and said, "*Que viva! Un varón!* Hurrah, a boy!" Dad was so tired driving home that he fell asleep at the wheel. Suddenly, he dreamed that he saw a woman and a burro crossing the road. He slammed on the brakes and found he had stopped right before hitting the "control," the toll post across the road.

After Bob was born, my mother's best friend and fellow missionary "Aunt" Betty took Jan and me up to Picalquí for a few days. We took the *autocarril,* a trolley car that ran on the railroad track. Aunt Betty had packed a lunch for us, and we felt so grown-up sitting on the seats with her and looking out the windows at the mountains and canyons and the villages we passed. The trip to Picalquí by car was a long, dusty road with many, many curves through the mountains. The train track was also winding, along steep cliffs where the cliff rose on one side and dropped off on the other. Just as we were passing through a tunnel, we heard a screeching, smelled smoke, and felt a jolt: the car had jumped the track. Thank goodness it was in the tunnel, or we might have ended up at the bottom of the canyon. Other children were crying, but Jan and I were brave and didn't cry. While the conductor and some of the passengers worked to get the car back on the track, the two of us and Aunt Betty started walking with some of the other passengers. When they got the car back on the track, they picked us up. Aunt Betty sent Mom a telegram so that she would know that we were safe, but I don't think Mom had even heard that there was a derailment.

This evening of my arrival, after we have eaten the rhubarb pie and are sipping our tea, I ask Mercedes about her own childbirth experiences. Having recently passed the modern maternity hospital, I am aware that births are managed much differently now than they were when I grew up here in Ecuador. Seeing this hospital has made me realize the vast changes that have occurred in this country just in my own lifetime. Mercedes tells me that all four of her children were born in cold, sterile delivery rooms at the local maternity clinic. She shares a wish that the traditional way of birth might be somehow combined with the safety of modern medicine.

"What was that traditional birth like?" I ask. "I remember my father and mother being called out to a home when something went wrong, a breech or a stillborn. But I don't know much about traditional birth. Please tell me." I want to better understand this culture surrounding my childhood, yet not of my childhood. And what woman doesn't want to talk about that wonderful moment when a baby arrives?

She settles back. "In the home where the mother is awaiting a baby, there is much advance preparation of the one room—there is only one bedroom in the house. There must always be an *estera*."

"A what?" I ask.

"A mat woven from reeds. There always should be an estera. Blankets are put on the mat to make it soft. In the kitchen, water is heating. As the water heats, it warms up the environment, the two rooms of the house—the kitchen and the bedroom. When the area is nice and warm and the mother herself knows that labor has started, she kneels and is supported by whatever will support her."

"Kneeling?" I ask. I think of the sterile sheets on modern hospital beds, the women I saw as a nurse, apprehensively waiting in the beds. Lying down, always lying down.

"Yes, that's the way it has been done for thousands of years, I suppose. The husband is always there to support her while she kneels. The other children generally are not allowed." She considers a moment.

"So someone takes them to another house?"

"Someone takes them outside. But, you know, they are hanging around outside, eager to see everything. The only person permitted in the room is a familiar woman assisting the midwife, who is directly responsible. The friend is preparing clean clothes to receive the baby and castor bean leaves. You remember castor beans, right? We used to string them together and use them for light."

I nod. "They grew wild along the paths where we played," I say.

"Well, the fire is ready with the hot water and the castor bean leaves are spread out to receive the infant. As soon as the baby falls onto the leaves, it is wrapped completely and bathed. Meanwhile, someone is waiting for the placenta. When the placenta is delivered, the umbilical cord is cut with the sharp edge of some ribbon grass, after it is tied, of course."

Outside of the house, a rooster crows. The chickens and rooster are finding their perches for the night in the tree behind the house. Raising chickens has been an income supplement for many of these families for ages. Mercedes stops for a moment, then smiles and goes on. "The mother is cleaned up with the hot water and wrapped up completely so that she does not get cold for anything in the world. Then the mother is allowed to lie down, and they bring the baby, all bathed and dressed, to the mother. From then on, they are always together. The father is also there, along with everyone else who lives in the house. The nourishment for the mother is *cuy*, guinea pig soup, because they want her to have lots of babies, to be very fertile."

"Yes, and the cuy, the cuy has lots of babies." Then I begin to think about it. "Guinea pig soup? I remember being given roasted cuy, but I don't think I ever had it in soup."

"In soup, in soup. Never roasted. She also needs to eat white carrots in the soup. To purify her blood, she has to drink teas made with about fifteen to seventeen kinds of herbs. We call them purgative waters, so that she will not have any clots remaining in her uterus."

"Were blood clots in the womb that common?" I ask. The nurse in me wants all the details.

Mercedes shakes her head. "Not if the woman drank the herbal teas," she says. "The baby is bathed in water with an herb called ñakjchasisa to prevent rashes. Then it is wrapped tightly with a *faja*, or woven belt, with his head in a good position." She folds her napkin into a triangle to show me. "Two cloth triangles are used: one to keep his head warm and the other like a scarf around the baby's neck to keep his head upright. That way, the baby can develop his hearing and vision because he is always quiet, never startled by a jerking arm or leg. Because he is tightly wrapped, he sleeps well."

In our modern American hospital nurseries, we are just rediscovering how swaddling babies helps to sooth them so they relax and sleep. "And how soon does the mother get up?" I wonder. That has been a topic evolving in the States for decades.

"The mother rests for at least thirty days, not bathing, not getting chilled. Temperature is very important." Thirty days! Imagine! I really am curious about each part of the story. Mercedes shares each detail as a gift from the treasured store of traditions that she and her people have come to value.

"Is there someone in the house to help the new mother?" I am remembering the births of my two daughters and how much it meant to me to have my mother come to help. And I think of all those children who were waiting outside the house during the birth.

"The mother-in-law, the mother or a sister of the mother's stays to help. The mother only eats hot food—never drinking any cold water or eating anything cold. And strengthening with meat. New mothers should eat chicken or that guinea pig soup every day brought in by friends or relatives."

"It all seems to be so much more people-oriented than our sterile birth places," I say. "We generally keep people at arm's length. There are even masks now and sanitizers."

"I know. But here friends and extended family come to visit. All are welcome—sort of an open house. The baby is handed to each visitor to receive a blessing. Then that person becomes a godparent, always responsible for the baby. That is called *sarushka* in Kichwa. At the moment the woman visitor is handed the baby, she is called *achima*. It means she was one of the people who visited the baby when it was born, and for the rest of her life, she is *achi*, she is always greeted as achima. The achima gives the baby a chicken or a little chick to raise so that he will have income, or a little pig. The child grows up with a whole community of godparents."

"So for that reason the child is raised by the whole community." I think of the African saying "It takes a whole village to raise a child." I ask her to tell me more. None of this was part of my experience when I was a missionary child. But the rich cultural traditions feed my soul.

Dusk has settled over the little community. The warm scent of the steamed humitas lingers in the house. "After a baby is born, no one can come to visit after sunset at six. It was thought that the devil came out to wander the paths, so they did not want a visitor to bring any evil spirits. For the same reason children are not allowed to play outside after six. Everyone is home going to bed."

Mercedes smiles, remembering. I imagine that she has been describing the births of herself and her brothers Enrique and Raul to the very young couple, her parents Pedro and Maria, so many years ago. "But it is so different now," she goes on. "After we became modern, I had my children in a maternity clinic. It was so cold there that I trembled terribly, stretched out on the bed. And that thin hospital gown, not like home. We did not treat our children in the traditional way either because we thought it wasn't good. We never wrapped them in the faja, so they grew up alone in a crib. But the way of our ancestors was to never leave the baby alone, never. In spite of that, you didn't see any dependency, none."

"Because they felt secure…"

"They were always with their mother or father, even as they grew up. They were carried to work. If the mother had to carry a load, she carried the baby in front, and as the child grew, he would be placed at the edge of the field. He would be playing, but the whole time, looking at his mother and the other people who were working. Never alone. I think that is why we, as a people, are so energetic, so brave."

We hear Fabian's truck in front of the house, and Ernesto bursts through the gate and into the house in his soccer uniform from late practice. He is ready for me to join him in building a Lego house before going to bed.

It has been a long, long day, but rewarding. Like women everywhere, Mercedes and I have shared the details of our birth experiences—of being born, of giving birth. We are two little girls who played with dolls together, now adults with children and grandchildren of our own. Births in the same world, yet worlds apart. I have thought that our lives have followed parallel paths. My brother says, though, that perhaps it was our souls that had traveled parallel paths. As we embark on this journey of remembering, I believe he may be right.

Chapter 4
Washing Days

The next morning, as Mercedes drives me around the village to orient me, I see there is now a bridge across the Quebrada Grande, big ravine, connecting Llano Chico to Llano Grande. There is barely a trickle of water running along the bottom of the canyon. But I remember when the Quebrada Grande was the hub of women's work in the community. This was where they washed their clothes, seeming to enjoy the process.

It was not always enjoyable for me. When our children were small, we liked to listen to the record of "Free to be, you and me," where Carol Channing told a story about TV commercials for cleaning supplies. These words so reflected my own dismal feelings about doing housework. I usually warned my children to stay clear of me on cleaning day because my fuse was so short.

Remember, nobody smiles doing housework
but those ladies you see on TV.
Your mommy hates housework.
Your daddy hates housework.
. . . housework is just no fun.

When I compare two experiences of washing day from my childhood in Ecuador—one, the Kitu Kara women of Llano Grande laughing together, and the other, the missionary women who lived alongside them in the same community working in a solitary way—the words of Carol Channing ring so true. In spite of how hard life was for the native Ecuadorian women, when it came to washing day in the quebrada, they did it together. The women beat the clothes on rocks while babies bounced about on their mothers' backs. Clean clothes were spread out to dry on the rocks and shrubs at the bottom of the quebrada, as children played while the women laughed and talked. How different from each missionary wife, doing her washing alone, even with the convenience of a washing machine, hot water, and soap. Alone in the kitchen, my mother cooked on a wood stove. She swept even the rugs with a broom, and the dust that settled on the furniture was unending. Washing clothes was another task that never seemed to end.

Recalling washing day in the mission gives me a chance to reconstruct our mission home in my mind. The laundry room was the first room one entered when coming into the house from the porch, unless a formal occasion required entering through the living room door. The white enameled washing machine would be pulled into the middle of the small room, next to the concrete sinks, and mountains of dirty clothes were piled around it.

A thirsty dirt road led from the Pan-American Highway past our house and down to the quebrada. Although the road could become a rushing torrent of mud in a downpour, usually it was dry and dusty. The sun beat down, baking the sand so that it burned our feet through the rubber soles of our tennis shoes. Scorpions and tarantulas could be found hiding in the dry weeds along the road, but usually it was lizards that we found. Wind rustled the weeds and lifted the dust from the road to blow it in our eyes and noses.

The mission farm was at the end of that dirt road, just before it descended into the quebrada. Although the image of missionaries typically is that of someone sharing the Gospel to groups of native people, often under a large tree, my parents' work was more varied. The Church of the Brethren that sent them had purchased a property where my father, an Illinois farm boy, and other North American missionaries farmed the land, demonstrating newer farming methods and helping to improve the local stock by introducing chickens, pigs, goats, sheep, and cows provided by Heifer Project (now Heifer International).

Our house had been an old hacienda house with thick adobe walls and a porch with four rooms, all leading off the porch. By the time we moved into it, the house had glass windows, a glass sunroom off the living room and an addition with a bathroom and three bedrooms that opened onto a large enclosed porch. The outside walls were covered with crème-colored stucco and the floors were wood and tile, and along the front porch my mother always planted sweet peas that climbed strings. An adobe and stucco wall surrounded the house. Outside the wall were a chicken house and a vegetable garden with a fig tree in the middle. We spent many hours climbing the huge, old tree and claiming specific branches as our own, so that when I learned about the Garden of Eden in Sunday school, I knew exactly what it looked like because we had just such a garden beside our house.

The house was one of several on the farm. Closest to the road was the hired man's house, a small, two-room house with a porch where we often gathered to shell corn together with him and his family and to play with his babies. Across the alfalfa field was a two-story missionaries' house that had two apartments, one opening on ground level where there was a porch and a one-room clinic and the lower opening out over the hillside, the woods, and the quebrada. Between that house and the hired man's was the barn, a long, low adobe building with a porch over which a loft was used to dry and store alfalfa. The cows came into the barn to be milked, and the sheep and goats lived in corrals in front of the barn.

Building all of this had required water. Water was in scarce supply. When the church first selected Llano Grande for their mission, the need for water was a primary concern. In a report dated January 1946, Dad wrote, "The matter of water is a difficult one as we have mentioned before. There is none on the place, even for household use, or drinking. It is necessary here to petition the government for the right to take water out of the natural ravines…If refused water rights, then we may need to try wells and cisterns. The rainfall is very small in the region, but we do not know exactly how small as yet." The mission finally settled on cisterns to collect rainwater from the eaves for our water supply.

Until the community got the water pipe and faucet at Cuatro Esquinas, Four Corners, where the two main dirt roads in the community intersected, all the water that people used had to be carried up from the quebrada. Although the word quebrada translates to "ravine," it was really more of a canyon. Erosion had worn it deep into the volcanic rock, and the sides were steep in both directions with paths leading down one side and up the other. There was no bridge at that time, so to go to Llano Chico, the village on the other side, one needed to walk down the steep path and then climb the other side. Few ventured this journey at night because the stones and rocks could slide your feet right out from under you. If you strayed from the path, you could plunge precipitously onto the boulders at the bottom, and a sudden downpour could cause a flash flood that turned the trickle of water at the bottom into a deadly roaring torrent. I remember more than once during a downpour when frantic parents knocked on our door asking Dad to help rescue their child who was stranded in the quebrada with sheep. Once Dad found the terrified little boy hanging from a root, holding a lamb, the rest of the herd washed down the river.

Before the cistern was built on the farm, when they were remodeling the old hacienda house that became our home, a hired man with a burro had to carry water up to the farm. A wooden frame sat on the burro's back as sort of a saddle with two wooden barrels loaded onto the frame. The burros were small, the loads were heavy, and the path was steep. These animals with floppy ears and white muzzles had broad backs and short legs that were able to carry more water at a time than the men and women who carried their daily water to their homes in large clay jars. In this dry country, the quebrada's small stream of melted snow running through the bottom of the deep ravine was the only source of water for the hard-working people of the local, native community.

The road in front of our house was the main route by which people could access the stream. Early in the morning and near sunset, we would hear the little boys who herded sheep walking by with their animals, playing their *rondadors* (pan pipes). The boys blew down into a series of reeds that formed the "national instrument" of Ecuador, and as their mouths moved over the reeds, the hollow sounds melded to create repetitive tunes that accompanied the rhythmic beating of their bare feet against the dirt. The lilting music contrasted with the repetitive monotony that was their lives. Pigs were herded with long branches, and the pigs were always trying to go into the paths of passing cars, the opposite direction from where they were being shooed, terrifying their small attendants.

Women passed with bundles of clothes and water jars suspended from straps over their foreheads. On the way back, they might also stop in the woods to pick up kindling for their fires. They looked like moving trees with the long sticks and many branches strapped to their backs. Somewhere in all of this there was also usually a baby tied in a large, white carrying cloth on its mother's back or nursing at her breast. Even walking up the road with their loads, women and girls were still hard at work, never idle, always spinning wool while they walked. The wool was tied to a eucalyptus stick that they carried in one hand. In the other hand was a spindle made from a ribbon grass spike and a small round weight. As they walked they spun the yarn and wound it on the spindle, and when they stopped to move the baby, shoo their other children, or pick up wood, they tucked the stick and spindle under one arm. Always moving, always working.

While our neighbors worked, we missionary children played in these same woods. Jim and John, the sons of the missionary agronomist, lived in the other mission house and were our constant companions. In denim bib overalls, tee shirts and black canvas high-top sneakers (or sometimes barefoot), we played on the same rocky, dry hillsides where little boys watched their family's sheep while they played their rondadors. Sometimes we made arrows with the same ribbon grass spikes that were used for spinning and bows from the green boughs of the eucalyptus trees.

We would walk down to the quebrada. The smell of dust and eucalyptus was heavy in the air, and the sun beat down as we walked. The path soon narrowed so that we needed to walk single file much of the way. In spite of all the foot traffic on the path, it was still steep, and loose rocks sometimes sent us sliding. Giant agave-like *cabuyas* lined the path along the side of the quebrada. Gray-blue, hard, fleshy, waxy leaves with thorns on their edges and a longer thorn on the tip were distributed like a rosette around a low center trunk on this plant, and these succulent, thorny leaves reached out to scratch us if we got too close. If we broke off the thorn at the tip, some of the fibers came along, and we pretended we were going to use it for sewing or we'd use it to carve our initials into the broad, waxy leaves. The cabuyas were large enough to provide shade if we needed to rest. The fibers from these spectacular plants also served for making rope, gunnysacks, bags, and the soles for the *alpargatas* (sandals) that Leonidas, who lived across the road from us, was expert at making.

> From an article in the Church of the Brethren archives ...
>
> ### The Unfolding
> Ruby Rhoades   Quito, Ecuador
>
> When artists wish to paint a typical Indian scene, they never fail to include a cabuya plant. It is a sturdy, straight, heavy plant with a hard center. From the center each long leaf breaks away, leaving the zigzag mark that outlines its pointed edges. For the long lifetime of the plant, each leaf carries the marks of the one which preceded and the one which followed it.
>
> Fascinated, one could study the plant for hours. But watching the unfolding of a new leaf, I find myself comparing that plant with the unfolding of the church's work here in this valley. That work has hardly opened at all yet, but there are those marks, clear and understandable.
>
> Maybe the first ones go back to the big fiesta on Easter. Another leaf started to pull away when the carpenter asked privately to buy a Bible. It must have been happening as he walked up the road to his home, with the Bible hidden under his coat. It must have given just a bit more each time he turned another page, reading alone by candlelight.
>
> Today another leaf is tugging at the heart of the plant. You see, on Sunday the priest prohibited the reading of the Bible and asked the parishioners to band together in destruction of the Bibles already in their hands, and cooperation in the destruction of this thing that can so damage the people. The carpenter still wished to continue Bible instruction but asked that it be in secret.
>
> The heart of the plant is hardly touched. But, oh, the inadequacy we feel as we watch the markings, so permanently placed on these first leaves. Our prayer, and we ask you to pray with us, "Give us strength, wisdom, courage and faith that Thy will may be done in this land."

Now, as Mercedes and I drive up the two-lane, paved road, the way is still steep and winding. But there are few cabuyas, and the eucalyptus trees that used to form the woods are now just a scattering of trees along the hillside. The only reason to go down this winding road is to cross the bridge and go up the other side on the way into Quito. Yet, looking up the ravine, I am taken back to the scene of washing day so long ago.

With their babies bobbing on their backs, the women beat their clothes on the rocks, using the juice from a cabuya leaf, which they beat on the rocks until the liquid separated from the fibers, as soap. Then they spread the clothes out on the large rocks to dry in the sun—men's short white cotton pants, women's white blouses covered with bright embroidery, and small children's shirts and panties. While the clothes dried, the women and girls, in just their slips, bathed in the water, loosing their braids and letting the long, black hair fall over their heads as they leaned into the pools of water. Sometimes, there was a bar of soap, but usually it was the cabuya leaves again. They laughed and talked in Kichwa, the ancient Inca language that we never learned. Children chased each other along the edge of the stream. As they stared at the little white children passing by, the native children pointed and called out, "*Gringo, piringo, pata de shamingo.*" Women would turn to one another and whisper things in Kichwa. Were they talking about us?

At Cuatro Esquinas, we park at a small *tienda* or "mom-and-pop" grocery. We stop and get out. The door is closed, but we can hear movement inside. Mercedes calls out to the woman inside who, she tells me, is an old neighbor of hers. An older woman in a wool skirt and bare feet opens the door. Mercedes goes in to buy some bananas and cheese and a chunk of laundry soap while I wait on the sidewalk and watch the faces passing by, the straight black hair, the soft brown skin, and the high cheekbones. They have a warm, familiar feel though I do not know a single one of them today.

As I look back now, I realize that while these native Ecuadorians lived as neighbors, in close proximity, their lives were still foreign to us. Although I took for granted the comforts we enjoyed in our remodeled *hacienda* house, on a farm which we and the community called Bella Vista, I also imagined being part of this close-knit community where most of the people were related and looked out for one another. Yet, it seems that the very comforts I took for granted but which were so foreign to their way of life were what kept me always an outsider.

As the missionary wives did their washing, what they lacked in the camaraderie I saw in the ravine they made up for in modern conveniences. On each return trip from the States, we brought things like laundry soap, canning jars, boxes of Jell-O, and enough children's shoes to last four years. The shoe store in my mother's hometown actually measured our feet and estimated how they would grow over the next four years. The supply of children's shoes would be packed into metal drums with metal tops and shipped to Ecuador for us. Once, when a puzzled customs officer looked quizzically into a packed drum filled with children's shoes, my mother patted her then-pregnant belly and said, "Mucho baby."

The rainwater collected from the mission's downspouts was run from the cisterns through plumbing pipes into the house. Washing was a solitary process for the missionary wives. As with the women in the quebrada, their husbands were busy with work, and the washing fell to the women. Missing her extended family back in the States, my mother may have found the work lonely and tedious; after all, she had left her family in Indiana to come to Ecuador with her husband and children to answer a call to ministry that she had felt since childhood. Now she found herself laboring at home while my father made pastoral calls on the villagers or worked the hard, dry land. And we had so many more clothes than the women in the quebrada. They washed clothes in their slips because they did not have a change of clothes to substitute while what they were wearing dried, but we four children could create mounds of dirty clothes for our mother to wash.

Pipes that circulated through the cook stove also heated the water, with the hot water tank built into the wall behind the stove. Dad would start the fire before leaving to visit homes in the community. He was about the important work of being a missionary. Mom needed to keep the fire going by adding wood to the stove, periodically feeling the tank to see if the water was hot enough.

Although we had running water, the water level in the cistern often got low and we had to conserve water by reusing it for the many loads of laundry, just adding more hot water as it cooled. This was the same process we used for baths, the cleanest person getting into the tub first and then the next cleanest. The youngest kid was last to bathe, in gray, lukewarm water, which was still warmer than the clear, melted snow the local people used to bathe in the quebrada. The addition of a little hot water made the bath water stretch for a family of six to bathe twice a week.

The dirty clothes were sorted according to color, with the whites being washed before the darker clothes, since the same water was used for all the loads. The space was small, and the only way to the rest of the house from the porch door was through the piles of laundry. Woe to the kid who tracked dirty feet through the piles! With a long day ahead of washing and hanging clothes on the line, Mom's patience was short, and the hairbrushes and paddles were handy for spanking transgressors. Being the oldest and most obedient, I was rarely on the receiving end of the paddle, but Bobby, the youngest and the only boy, recalls feeling like Mom was always spanking him with something.

Mom filled the washing machine with very hot water from the tank and added shaved bar soap. On one side of the tub was the lever that allowed you to engage or disengage the agitator. Since the washer was on wheels, it moved around the laundry room when the agitator was churning the clothes. A hose at the bottom allowed the used water to drain into a hole on the floor that led through the wall to the yard outside. Mom dipped clothes out of the hot water with a thick eucalyptus stick and put them through the wringer, which could be swung over the wash tub so that extracted wash water would fall back into the tub to be reused for the next load or over one of the cement sinks filled with rinse water. A user's fingers, hand, arm, or hair could become entangled in the laundry being squeezed, resulting in horrific injuries; unwary bystanders, such as children, could also be caught and hurt. If the pile of wet clothing was too thick, the ringer did pop open. Although it had this safety feature, Mom usually did not let us help and rarely even allowed Maria, the young local woman who helped with housework, to help with the washing. It was Mom's solitary, monotonous task.

"Monday, wash day"

I recall one such washing day. I am standing in the doorway to the porch. Above is a plaster ceiling with some fly specks. The bare lightbulb is on because washing day is the one time the mission electric generator is turned on during the day to run the washing machines. All the missionary wives do their washing on the same day. Under my feet is the smooth tile floor—black and white squares, with piles of sorted laundry sitting around. Behind the door to my left are pegs with Dad's work shirts, some hats and a pith helmet that I never see him wear, and a shotgun, only taken down when there is a rabid dog loose in the community. A window to my right faces the front yard with its dry, weedy lawn. The only part of the yard that is ever green is around the drain where the wash water runs out after washing day. There are flies batting against the inside of the window and some dead ones on the windowsill. Mom is always on the prowl for flies, usually with a folded *Gospel Messenger* magazine. Not having grown up on a farm, she never could get used to all the flies that come along with raising chickens, pigs, and cows.

Behind me the screen door is pulled shut by a stretchy band of rubber from an old tire inner tube. That door is opened and closed so often that it really doesn't keep out many of the flies. My straight, wispy blond hair brushes my face, blowing from the wind that always comes through the screen door. In front of me, beside the washing machine and concrete sinks, stands my mother in her apron, always in her apron, tall and beautiful, with clear plastic-rimmed glasses. Her shoulder-length, curly brown hair is pulled back stylishly with bobby pins, like the beauty queen she had been in high school. Her plaid cotton dress is starched and pressed, and she wears white cotton anklets and brown penny loafers. She sighs as she lifts the next load of clothes into the washer.

I listen to the washing machine, beating back and forth rhythmically. The lever that turns the agitator on and off is clunking away, and the radio is playing since the electricity was on. Is it HCJB Christian programming, broadcasting from high in the Andes? Or is it the popular music of Patience and Prudence singing "I know you belong to someone else. But tonight, you belong to me," which Mom enjoyed having on when we were back in the States? And there is also the buzzing of those ever-present flies that seem to be attracted to the smells of warm food and fresh fruit from the kitchen and anything we children dropped on the floor. The strongest smell is the Ivory or Fell's Naphtha she shaves off the bars to use for washing, and there is also the scent of bluing she uses to rinse the whites.

My cotton tee shirt is scratchy from being dried on the line. The floor is cool under my feet, bare now that we have gotten back from the quebrada. We are the only missionary kids allowed to go barefoot, and we are also the ones who were treated annually for hookworm. Didn't anyone tell my parents how you get hookworm? Or did they just want to allow us to feel the freedom of doing as we pleased? They also allowed us to eat the garlicky, roasted guinea pigs that people brought us and to carry the native babies on our backs, like the local women, though we then needed to be treated for lice. And Mom wears lipstick, which most missionary wives do not. Once, when some more conservative missionaries dropped in unannounced on a Sunday afternoon, they even found Coke bottles, bowls of popcorn kernels, and cards all over the living room floor. The cards were Rook cards, "missionary bridge," but cards nonetheless when the Bible explicitly said you shouldn't gamble or at least not "wager." This is home as I know it.

To me, that home felt warm and secure, like I belonged. But there was no accounting for the way my mother's pain and loneliness would be expressed as it was this washing day. Spanking was an accepted form of discipline in most homes at that time. Although it might be an expression of anger or frustration, it was particularly handed out for misbehaving in front of other people. My mother's own experience of growing up a preacher's kid only reinforced her belief that missionary kids should always look well behaved, and the freedom we experienced playing in the woods disappeared completely when we were being visited by people from the city or from the mission board. Arguing in front of visitors was followed by a spanking with a hairbrush or ping pong paddle.

So the day came when Bobby hit Mom with the laundry stick. He recalls that he had had enough of being smacked with whatever object Mom found handy. She had spanked him for walking through the piles of laundry with feet muddy from playing by the drain in the yard. Red-faced and angry, after one too many spankings, he followed her into the laundry room. "I want to hit you!" he screamed. To our surprise, she replied, "Here is a stick," and handed him the stick she was using to dip the clothes from the water. We watched in horror, almost slow motion. Hitting our powerful, angry mother was just unthinkable. "No, Bobby, no!" We held our breath and watched as he defiantly hit her leg with that stick. He was little more than a toddler, and her skirt cushioned the blow, so it was not pain that registered but surprise. She was as shocked as we were, looking on. Bob recalls now that she never again offered to let him hit her, though he still got spankings himself.

I don't remember seeing children being hit around the community, though wife beating was commonplace. Perhaps the communal work and shared child care helped to buffer the pressures the native women felt, or perhaps they just accepted all of the burden as part of their lot in life. Still, I wonder if my mother would have been more patient if she had been sharing the washing time with some other mothers. Perhaps, if we had been with other children, we would not have been so demanding. If we could have been close to our mother while still playing freely with our friends, we would not have been tramping through piles of unwashed laundry.

> *So, little boys, little girls,*
> *If you want all the days of your lives*
> *To seem sunny as summer weather,*
> *Make sure, when there's housework to do,*
> *That you do it together!*

Mercedes comes out of the tienda with a small plastic bag of groceries. She will not need to go to the quebrada to wash her clothes. All the homes in the community now have running water. She washes clothes at the concrete washboard behind her house and hangs them to dry on clotheslines stretched between her house and Elizabeth's house. It is not like the work of her mother, but housework still consumes a large part of her day. She does it willingly.

Chapter 5
Heather Ann

I enjoy having my Ecuadorian friends like Mercedes and her welcoming family to visit while I am here. They connect me to my past. But there were others who also made up a significant part of my childhood community—the group of missionaries who gave us a sense of family, of belonging. Most of the missionaries who made up my *true* extended family are no longer in Ecuador. Many are no longer living. These were the people who became uncles, aunts, and cousins to us when our biological family members back home were virtual strangers, and among the closest to us were Aunt Betty and her family.

When my younger sister Becca was three and I was almost eight, Becca had vaginal cancer. I always heard about how all the churches in the denomination were praying for her healing. When we were on furlough visiting the churches that supported our mission, women were always coming up to me and my two sisters and asking, "Which is the little girl who was so sick? We were praying for her." Jan and I gladly pointed to Becca because it meant she would get a kiss from some good church lady.

Although the doctors at Mayo Clinic initially said that it would be futile, my mother eventually convinced them to operate. Becca is still alive and cancer-free, and people still recall the power of prayer in her healing.

Before Becca was born, my mother had also prayed for another little girl, the daughter of her best friend in Ecuador, a little girl whose birth my mother had eagerly awaited while my mother herself awaited the birth of my sister Jan. I'm not so sure about prayer being able to change the mind of the Almighty. But Mom believed she had changed God's mind about sparing the life of our friends' little girl. Heather Ann did live, but her birth left her blind and profoundly mentally handicapped, with spasticity and seizures.

After Heather Ann was born, Mom would say, "I prayed so hard that God would spare Heather's life. I wonder now if God's plan had been for Heather to die and our prayers changed His mind, only to leave her with profound disability. Was it really right to pray so hard?" I tend to believe that faith in God helps us walk through our toughest times and come out better for it. Sometimes those tough times have a ripple effect far beyond what we might imagine.

My earliest experience with a child with severe disabilities was Heather Ann, though I had no idea what it really meant to be disabled. Heather felt more like a friend than someone special. She was between my sister Jan and me in age, and we always imagined being able to play with her. We desperately wanted a near-by cousin, a peer with whom we could play and share our secrets, another little girl who knew our experience of living in this beautiful country but not really belonging. Although Heather was able to be present with us when we played, she could not play, talk, or even see. So I named my doll Heather Ann. When I played with my doll, I pretended that I was playing with Heather.

Adult missionaries were addressed by the children as "Aunt" or "Uncle." When Aunt Betty went into labor, the family was living in Picalquí, high in the Andes Mountains. The Pan-American Highway at that time was a winding, dusty cobblestone road full of hairpin curves and narrow passages along mountainsides. My mother called the highway a washboard because it jostled travelers who ventured there. Our friends' means of transportation was an old army truck with an open cab, and I can only imagine the agony of making that trip deep in the throes of labor. I think Heather was lying crossways in Aunt Betty's womb and the labor was hard. Like my sister Jan, who would be born later that year, Heather was born at our house. This was Aunt Betty's first baby, and the young missionaries were new to Ecuador. When they arrived at our house, Betty's water had already broken and she was in a lot of pain. A doctor and nurse were summoned to assist with the birth there in my parents' bedroom.

From my later experience as a labor and delivery nurse, I know this kind of delivery is the birth attendants' worst nightmare. The doctor would have had to use his hands to reach into the womb and grasp the baby's legs and pull her around. It would have been especially painful for Aunt Betty because it would have been without anything for the pain or to help her uterus relax. Heather arrived limp and lifeless, and when she did not breathe, the nurse swung her by the legs to try to get her to breathe and dislocated Heather's hip. Aunt Betty believes that Heather was blind because they gave her oxygen to help her breathe, but I know now the blindness was more likely caused by the lack of oxygen to her newborn brain at the beginning.

Aunt Betty was my mother's best friend. Mom was outside the bedroom door, fervently praying that Heather would not die. Heather did not die, but she always would live with severe brain damage.

From a letter Dad wrote to the Mission Board: January, 1948

Dear friends,

…At the present time, we feel especially for the Paul S family of the United Andean Mission here. Their first baby, born in our home in Quito a year ago, suffered birth injuries leaving irreparable damage on the brain and nervous system. Two months ago, Mrs. S took the baby to New York for examination and treatment, if treatment were possible. Beside the nervous system damage, the baby has a dislocated hip and for that will need to remain in the United States in a cast for eight months. Paul is torn between going home and remaining on the field for the present. But he knows that, with only another family on the field, his work is urgently needed and that his board is financially unable to replace him now. We hope and pray that something satisfactory may be worked out for them in this time of trial. Their mission cooperates very well with ours and we have found real fellowship with them, though located at some distance from us. …

Sincerely,
Benton Rhoades

When I was about four or five years old, Mom decided that I was old enough to go spend time with Aunt Betty and Uncle Paul in Picalquí. I wonder that Mom was able to share her little girl with Betty, who had so enthusiastically looked forward to having a little girl to raise and now was caring for a severely disabled child. I cannot even imagine sending one of my young children on a trip away for several days! Perhaps Betty and Mom were so close that Mom was willing to send her oldest child to share with her friend.

Mom helped me pack my things and instructed me to be a good girl. "Do what Aunt Betty tells you to do. Don't leave your things lying around. Don't make a mess. Help with Heather and Davie…" I traveled with a missionary who was going up to Picalqui. I was dressed in a plaid cotton dress and anklets with brown shoes, my hair pulled into two ponytails with rubber bands. On my lap, I held my doll Heather Ann. I remember sitting between the missionary and an Ecuadorian man, neither of whom I really knew, through the long and dusty trip in the open cab of the old army truck. Squeezed in between them and the gearshift, I could barely see out the windshield. Well, actually, what I saw was the sky and a few distant mountains and the dust rolling up from the road. I was frightened, hungry, and really needed to pee, but when the men would ask me how I was doing, I would just nod and say "Fine."

Aunt Betty was excited to have a little girl visit and had planned activities for us to do together. She had been a high school cheerleader and was always urging others to cheer along with her. I remember my mother saying she wished she had as much enthusiasm as Betty, always coming up with fun ideas and getting everyone to sing along with her nonsense songs. Yet, her daughter told me when we were adults that her mother had always battled depression. I suppose the cheerleading was her way of coping.

While Aunt Betty excitedly told me all she had planned for my visit, she put my things in the room I would share with David, who was a baby. I had no sooner arrived than her cheerleading began. Right away, she wanted to get started with all she had anticipated, and she asked me if I wanted to listen to records. I obliged because my mother told me to be a good girl, but what I really wanted was to pee. The little record player played nursery rhymes and Little Golden Book songs like the "Saggy Baggy Elephant."

"One, two, three. Kick. One, two, three, kick," the little elephant sang. The picture showed him drinking water and lolling in a pool of water with his round little belly sticking up, and I could feel my belly round from the water I drank before leaving home. As I tried to concentrate on the songs, the pressure in my bladder increased. I didn't know where to find the bathroom and was afraid to ask permission. If a grownup said I should listen to records, then that's what a good girl should do, so there in the living room by the record player, I wet on the floor. I started to cry, and Aunt Betty showed me the bathroom and helped me get into dry clothes. I suppose she had not thought to show me the bathroom since both of her children were still in diapers.

The former cheerleader was bubbling with fun ideas. We made sandwiches and had a picnic on the porch. I would wake up early and "read" books to David in his crib. Aunt Betty colored with me, and we cut shapes out of colored paper and pasted them onto other colored paper. I sat on a stool in the kitchen when Aunt Betty took the milk out of the pasteurizer, coming out with a great head of foam. She put the hot milk foam in a tin cup for me to drink, and we poured some into a little dish for the kittens that were begging around our feet. She laughed and talked as she enjoyed doing typical things with a typical little girl.

The house had a glassed-in porch full of huge houseplants. There among the plants one day, Aunt Betty got out what was then called a standing box and leg braces for Heather. "Let's help Heather learn to stand up," she said with her usual enthusiasm. The heavy braces were made of leather and steel with large buckles to hold them in place at her waist and knees. Brown, high-topped leather shoes were attached to the ends of the braces. The stander was a tall, green wooden box that opened at the front to allow Heather to be strapped in place. Heather was totally unable to cooperate as we laid her stiff little body down on the full-leg braces and buckled them into place. She arched and cried out when we hoisted her into a standing position; after a brief time in the standing box, we saw that she wasn't tolerating it and took her out. Aunt Betty looked deflated and defeated, but I felt so important to be able to help my friend.

Heather spent most of her time in a large wooden and wicker

wheelchair. She was blind, but she seemed to enjoy having people around her. She would laugh at the sounds of birds outside or the egg beater in the kitchen. Since she was not really able to eat from a spoon or drink from a cup, they gave her mashed food or a bottle. She would bite down on the spoon or nipple and thrust the food with her tongue, and large bibs were placed around her neck to catch the food and saliva that drooled from her mouth. As Aunt Betty went through her next pregnancy and worked as a teacher at the mission school, she also had to bathe and diaper her growing daughter. As Heather got bigger, Aunt Betty and Uncle Paul had to think about putting her in a nursing home, though it broke their hearts.

Aunt Betty told me later, "I didn't think I would ever be able to leave her." Heather's maternal grandmother thought it would be terrible for them to place her in a home, but she saw the true situation when she came to visit. When she tried to hold and cuddle Heather, Heather arched and bit down involuntarily on her shoulder.

Heather's grandmother had the same pained and disappointed look that I remember seeing on the faces of the families of two different little girls whom I cared for as a nurse when I worked at a large children's hospital. Both little girls were five years old and had been preparing to start kindergarten. One little girl had stopped breathing after a tonsillectomy and had suffered severe brain damage. Her mother tearfully told me, "The night before the surgery, a friend brought over some used school clothes, and Teresa tried on each one, twirling and dancing around the living room."

Now her daughter stared without looking, barely moving, arching her back and crying out loudly. When I visited her home after she left the hospital, her father was trying to sleep because he worked nights, and he shouted from the bedroom, "Keep her quiet so I can sleep." The mother silently wept.

The second little girl from another family had aspirated a grape and went without oxygen long enough that her brain was damaged. Because her parents only spoke Spanish, which I spoke fluently, I spent a lot of time sitting with them in the hospital room. While the parents sat numbly watching her limp form, her older sister recalled how excited Maya had been about starting kindergarten.

"She had her little backpack with the school supplies. She was so excited about riding the school bus with the other kids. Now she won't be able to go to school." By the time she came for follow-up as an outpatient, she was arching so much that it was hard to keep her in the wheelchair. Again, I looked into her parents' faces filled with pain, confusion, and sorrow.

Before Heather went to a nursing home, I remember her family coming for a holiday at our mission. They put Heather in her wheelchair on the large, sunny porch where we children were playing. Heather was wearing a plaid cotton dress with a pixie collar just like Jan and I wore. Her light brown hair fell in loose curls, except for the back of her head, where she had worn most of the hair away by arching against the back of the chair. I sensed how desperately Aunt Betty wanted her to be part of the group, and we wanted that, too. Not wanting to leave her out, we stayed on the porch and tried to play with her. We brought her toys, we tickled her and talked to her, making her laugh. When she chuckled, we all laughed, and she laughed even more. It felt good to see her respond to our efforts to help her have fun.

When Heather was six, her parents took her to live in a church-related nursing home in the States, where there were a lot of older ladies to make over her. Our lives went on without her, though I know she was deeply missed by her family.

Through this time, Aunt Betty continued her cheerleading. When I was about twelve, Aunt Betty and her family took my sisters and brother and me on an outing to a swimming pool in Alangasi, near Quito. Once we were loaded into the carry-all with our picnic and swimsuits and towels, Aunt Betty began to lead us in nonsense songs to make the time fly. Recently, around a campfire in the Poconos, my sisters and brother and I had again whooped with laughter as we recalled her singing, "If I had wings, then off I would fly; off to Alangasi. There in the water I would long abide, long abide. There I would stay 'til I died." There were others, too, about villains who "beat little babies on the head, 'til they were dead…" and "the big, bold desperado out of Colorado." I once tried singing some of these songs to my children, but my husband quickly stopped me. To him, they were more gruesome than fun.

All the laughter and bravado, no doubt, helped to cover the pain of loss. During that same trip to Alangasi in 1957, Aunt Betty also shared a photo of Heather that had arrived in the mail that week. We all "ooed" and "aahed" over how cute she looked and how she was growing up. In the picture, Heather was sitting in a wheelchair in shorts and a tee shirt. I saw similarities to other girls her age. I even searched what she was wearing for clues about how kids my age dressed in the States.

When Heather was about sixteen, her family received a telegram saying that she had died. I know that Aunt Betty grieved, though I did not see it. We were living in Illinois, far from all the memories of Ecuador.

Fifty-two years after Heather Ann's passing, I asked Aunt Betty's daughter if she thought Aunt Betty would be willing to talk with me about Heather. She said, "We try to get Mom to talk about Heather, but she never will. Perhaps if you call her, she will talk."

I called Aunt Betty in the retirement home in Tennessee where she now lives. And, yes, Aunt Betty did talk about Heather when I called her. She told me that Heather is buried behind the nursing home, along with the directors of the home. The family went to visit her grave whenever they were in the States, just as they had visited her when she was alive. She told me that Heather had seizures all the rest of her life. Aunt Betty had thought she would never be able to leave Heather in the States; it would be too difficult, though it was for the best. But Aunt Betty especially recalled Heather's laughter. She said Heather was a happy person who loved the sound of an egg beater and of birds.

Was part of God's plan for Heather the ripple effect that her life had on mine? Heather was my peer and my earliest friend. Although I would not have been able to put it into words, I rode for a while with Heather and Aunt Betty as they navigated the rough waters of disability. As I have tried to help other families navigate these same waters, perhaps the fact that Heather was one of my earliest friends has helped me to relate to them as more than patients, as someone's sister, best friend, cousin, or aunt, trying to find their way through the most lonely and difficult of times.

This tile-roofed house had fallen into disrepair before the Church bought it.

As our family stayed in Quito awaiting the completion of our Mission home, donkeys hauled water for the construction.

Map below, from a booklet done by my father, illustrates approximate national boundaries in South America in the 1950s. Just south of the Colombia/Ecuador line is the Calderon region, where the mission was located. It is on the equator.

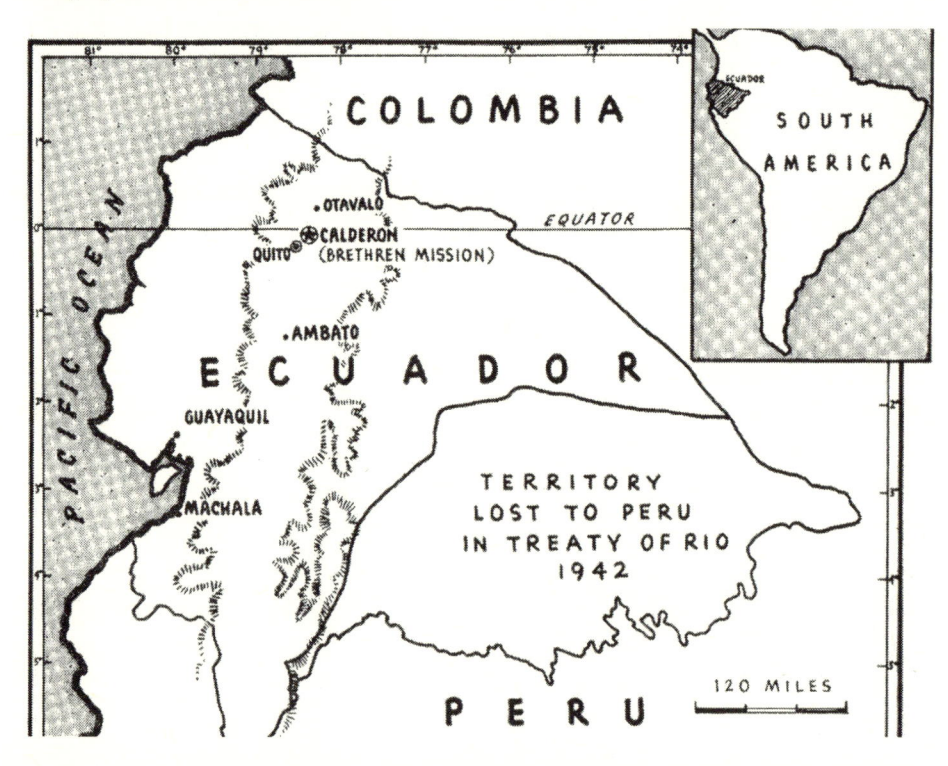

Newly repaired, this was our home.

Maria helped my mother. She is holding Bobby.

Jeannie, yearning for a friend, played with dolly Heather Ann.

Aunt Betty and Uncle Paul, here with Heather Ann, David, and Mica, were mainstays of the missionary community and our friends.

Jan and Becca in the quebrada. It went from dry to deluge.

Mom's photo notation called this cubuya a "cactus from which shoes are made." The sharp needle-like spines scratched us as we ran through the paths near our home.

I am getting my photo taken at Sunday school, standing (l to r) with Jan, Rosario Alobuela, Mercedes.

Chapter 6
Rain and My Tonsillectomy

On the third day of my visit, as I ride in the cab of the pickup truck over narrow, dirt roads in blinding rain, I remember the trip home from my tonsillectomy. I was five years old and riding in a truck as rain pattered on the windshield. Now that I am back in Llano Grande, sixty-five years after having my tonsils out, I see so much that feels the same.

First, today: it is the start of the rainy season, and people are anxious to get their crops in before the ground gets too wet for planting. My friend Mercedes has gone to the family property at the far end of the community to plant corn, a different field from the one where we picked corn the first day. Since I am staying at the home of her daughter Elizabeth and son-in-law Fabian, we do some things together. After eating our lunch of fried fish and manioc, we decide to take some lunch to Mercedes out in the field. The day has been sunny so far, but it is starting to cloud up, so we change into boots and raincoats. We pile into the double cab truck, Elizabeth and Fabian in front, eight-year-old Ernesto and me in back.

We drive down the paving-stone streets, past the small grocery store from yesterday and the green grocer under a plastic tarp, buses and trucks, dogs and chickens, women with umbrellas for the sun or the eventual rain and a man pushing a brightly painted popsicle cart. This is Cuatro Esquinas, Four Corners, the main intersection leading into Llano Grande that, when I was a child, was a crossroad of two dirt roads and had only a chicharia on one corner and cabuya fence rows along all the rest of the intersection. Now the street has sidewalks and is lined with large, walled homes built with money the owners earned working as cooks and gardeners in Spain. On through the village, past flat-roofed houses with high walls topped with broken glass to deter break-ins. Watchdogs bark from the rooftops. Then the houses become farther apart and there are more fields. Finally, we leave the street and begin to wind along a narrow dirt road.

"This is more like the Llano Grande you remember," says Fabian with a wink. Yes, it is. Rolling hills, bare except for eucalyptus trees and cabuya fence rows. A few small houses sit back from the road. The brown earth is lumpy with small mounds of *cangahua*, referred as the "cement subsurface" of the soil. This almost impermeable soil was always a frustration to my father's attempts to plow with the single-blade plow pulled by a pair of oxen.

As we get close to the site, Fabian turns the truck around and backs down the rest of the way to the field, since it is impossible to turn around at the end of the road. Elizabeth gets out and helps to direct him between the edges of the road. "*Da le, da le*," while motioning with her hand. Literally, "Give it, give it." My dad always liked to joke about someone saying, "*Da le, da le. Ya le dió!*" "Give it, give it. Now you gave it!" as the driver crashes into the cliff side.

In the distance we can see Mercedes and her brother Enrique, wearing boots and straw hats with bags of seed over their shoulders, pushing planting sticks into the plowed soil and dropping in seeds. Tia Maria, Mercedes's ninety-one-year-old mother, who welcomed me on the day I arrived, now sits along the path, her crutch beside her. She still dresses in the traditional wrapped skirt with the woven belt, the embroidered blouse, the white shawl with black stripes and the strings of beads around her neck. I know that she can see well, though she is quite deaf, so I hurry forward to greet and embrace her. When I get there, she says, "I've fallen and I can't get up." I try to help her up, but we need Fabian to help also. She says she came down with Enrique to watch them planting. After we get her back on her feet, she starts down a narrow path, using her crutch for support.

We too go down the hill to where Mercedes and Enrique are still planting. They stop only long enough for a well-mannered greeting because grey clouds are rolling in and they still have a lot of field to plant. The ground is soft from being plowed by the tractor, though rows vary with the contour of the hillside and from going around trees and shrubs. Enrique shows me how to push the planting stick into the soft soil, making a small hole into which I am to put two or three grains of corn and knock the soil over it with my boot. The sun is bright and I am glad for my hat. Down the row I go, digging holes, putting in seeds and covering them. We joke that this corn will be ready for humitas when I come back next year.

As I near the end of the row, I hear a gentle "plop" on the soft soil. The clouds have arrived and are ready to deliver their load of rain. I try to finish my row, as I feel the big drops of rain hitting my back and arms. The others are heading for the truck.

"Jeanne, come on. It's starting to rain."

I drop three seeds into the last hole and cover it, then start up the hill. The sky is dark and thunder rolls, with big drops turning instantly to sheets of rain. I hurriedly put my few remaining seeds into Enrique's bag and run to the truck as quickly as my boots allow through the freshly plowed rows. I throw my digging stick into the back of the truck and climb in beside little Ernesto and Tia Maria, who must have gotten into the truck before the rain began. They are not wet like the rest of us.

The cold rain and hail beat down on the cab of the truck as the windshield wipers beat back and forth. Inside the cab, all the wet bodies and warm breath quickly steam up the windows. The windshield is barely even cleared along the bottom by the defroster. Slowly we make our way up the steep, narrow road. Light reflects off the slick, clay-like congahua, and water runs in streams across the road at any low places. At other places, it carves out small gullies in the sand along the road.

I brush some of the fog from the window and stare out at the streams of water running down the hills, and I am back in the past, in the cab of that old International pickup with my parents, returning home after getting my tonsils out, the rain pouring down.

My parents had told me it was really special that I got to get my tonsils out in the presidential palace of Ecuador. They said the president had a nicer house in Quito, so he had moved the official offices to his home and turned the palace into a hospital.

They had plenty of time to prepare me. I had been having lots of sore throats and earaches. To get me ready for the operation, the doctor gave me a series of penicillin shots in his office. There weren't yet any books about going to the hospital, but I was told that I would be given ether to make me go to sleep. And when I woke up, I would get to eat ice cream. Not too bad, I thought.

Reality was another matter.

People dressed in white with white masks covering their faces took me away from my parents, wheeled me down a long, echoing hall into a big, cold room with bright lights. Then they held me down and put a mask on my face with a sharp, burning smell. I began to kick and scream, "Tell them I'll go to sleep without this. Tell them I'll go to sleep by myself." But my parents were way down the hall, and I was by myself among these strangers.

Once I was "asleep," I dreamed. My dreams alternated between a sailboat traveling around a globe of the earth and the doctors in a brightly lit room using popsicle sticks to take out my tonsils. Maybe the popsicle stick part had to do with the fact that my throat, when I woke up, felt like it had that time I chewed up a popsicle stick and got splinters in my throat.

I awakened in a high metal bed in the middle of a large, empty room. Across the room, on a rocking chair, sat the private duty nurse my parents had hired to stay with me. She came over and offered me a sip of water. That made me feel awful, and I vomited a stomachful of blood all over the bed and the nurse. I shivered with fear and then went back to sleep.

The next time I woke up, the nurse was making me something out of paper—there was a paper basket with something in it. "*Es un pollito*," she said. "It's a little chick."

I squinted at it. The beak was too wide. "*No, es un pato*." "No, it's a duck."

"*Un pollito*."

"*Un pato*."

She sighed and handed me her paper creation, whatever it was. She looked in her bag and pulled out a children's book, *Peter Rabbit* in Spanish, and read it to me. She brought me ice chips that felt good on my raw throat. No horrible bloody vomit. I went back to sleep.

When I woke up next, my parents were there. "Where is the ice cream?" I asked. Mom sent Dad right out to get some—and presents, the celluloid Kewpie doll I had admired in the market and some marbles in a little basket. I felt like a princess. They said that when I got home, I would get to eat baby food so that it wouldn't scratch my throat. Since I was the oldest and always helped feed my baby sister, it sounded really special to be the one eating baby food.

The next morning my parents arrived and dressed me in my own clothes. We left the hospital/presidential palace and got into the pickup truck for the ride home. The sun beat down on the truck and dust rolled up from among the cobblestones on the Pan-American Highway. It led us north out of Quito, past the Y in the road that could take us to the airport if we turned left. But we stayed to the right, toward Llano Grande. As we crested the hill and started down the five hairpin curves into the valley, black clouds gathered on the horizon.

At the bottom of the hill, we turned off the highway onto the dirt road to Llano Grande. Now big drops plopped onto the cab of the truck, and in no time sheets of rain poured down. The windshield wipers beat rhythmically back and forth. I repeated with their rhythm, "Rain, go there. Rain, go there." The windows fogged up, and Dad had to hunch down to see out of the part that the defroster succeeded in clearing. The truck skidded sideways in the slippery mud, and he had to work hard to keep it on the road as torrents of water rushed along both sides of the truck.

We finally reached Cuatro Esquinas and turned right, toward the mission. This road was sandy, and a hard rain always washed away the sand. Just before the farm, there was a big concrete culvert pipe for the Quebrada Chica, Little Ravine, to go under the road, and a rain like this was certain to cause the ravine to overflow the culvert. Sure enough, water was rushing over the road, and as Dad tried to drive through it the truck stalled. He took me out of the cab and carried me through the rushing water and up the hill to our house. From the safety of Dad's arms, the hail and rushing water did not feel so frightening.

At the house they wrapped me in towels and then in warm blankets. How they must have worried about my getting some kind of infection from being so wet and cold right after my operation. My sisters were waiting at the other missionaries' house, and since the rain had stopped, my parents took me over there. The kitchen was warm and supper was waiting. The fried chicken smelled so good; instead, I was brought a jar of baby food. I took one bite, and it tasted awful. I sat and stared at this jar of something unidentifiable while the others enjoyed fried chicken, mashed potatoes, and cooked carrots. There were fresh cookies for dessert, but I was not allowed these either because they might scratch my raw throat.

Then the other kids went out to play on the biggest piles of hail I had ever seen. Hail was the closest we ever got to snow, giving us visions of making a snowman. My chance was spoiled by having my tonsils out.

Today, in this similar foul weather, after being at Mercedes's farm, there are no piles of hail. But there are a few hailstones. The road hasn't washed out completely, but we do get soaked getting home.

Much has changed and much is still the same.

Chapter 7
Letters Home

I remember Mom sitting at the typewriter on a Sunday afternoon writing a letter "home." For me home was where my family was. Perhaps that was also true for Mom, but her family was geographically far away in Indiana, and my father's was in Illinois. Home for my mother would always be Indiana.

I believe my mother had wanted to be a missionary since she was a child. After her death, we found among her childhood mementos a small book of short stories her fifth grade class had written. The little book had covers of cardboard covered with grey fabric and was held together by two brass paper fastener brads. The word "Stories" and a tree were drawn on the cover in crayon. Inside, in purple mimeograph, were the words, "Book of Stories, Written by members of the FIFTH GRADE, CLIFTON CONSOLIDATED SCHOOL, Isabella Moulton Smith, Teacher." My mother had written a story about a little Chinese boy who became a Christian because of kind missionaries who brought him the "good news." The purple mimeograph has faded, but I could still make it out after eighty years.

> Little Chang
> By Ruby Frantz
>
> There was once a little boy who lived in China. They knew nothing of their kind Heavenly Father, and because of that they were not very good or kind. The little boy whom the story is about was named Chang.
>
> He often thought if only his mother would let him go to the Mission School he would be happy but it seemed as if she wouldn't. "I'd

be the best child. I'd help with the work and then I could teach Mother all I know," thought little Chang. Then there was a long pause. Chang was thinking. "I don't know—but maybe—I could run away. I know that isn't very nice but oh! I do want to so badly."

He had almost decided to do this when one day he heard someone talking to his mother. It was such a sweet, kind voice, and so loving that he knew it must be the missionary. Do you suppose that he was to go? He was thinking "If it could be, I'd be the very happiest boy in the world."

Just then he heard his mother say, "He's right in there. This way, Mrs." She continued, "I don't really want him to go to school, but I suppose if it is best for him, he'll have to go. He isn't a bit smart. He'll never learn much," she added.

"He can at least try," said the Missionary softly.

By that time they were now well into the room. Yes, it was then decided that he should go. His clothes were packed and he left at last. My, but he was glad. When he got there he was treated so kindly that he tried to be very, very good.

"The white people teach me everything," he said. "They teach me many hymns. My favorite hymn is 'Gentle Jesus, Meek and Mild'," he added.

He lived happily for several years among the missionaries, but finally came a sad day for him. The Missionary told him that it was time for him to go home. Little Chang cried and cried. "I can never be happy away from here," he wept.

"Why, child, don't cry, you know we've taught you a great deal and besides there are many other little children who want to learn these things, too," said the Missionary.

"Oh! But couldn't I be a helper in the kitchen or something?" he begged.

The Missionary whispered something to the other Missionary. "Yes. I think perhaps you can until I go. I am planning to go back to America and when you get big enough maybe you can take my place in this Mission School."

Chang was very happy and worked there, and no doubt he is today still a Missionary.

I don't know where my mother learned about missionaries in China at that early age, but I can imagine the Sunday school stories she may have listened to in the church basement, perhaps in a classroom behind a huge, blazing furnace. The teacher with her hair in a bun covered by a white net prayer covering may have even asked the children where they would want to go as missionaries. I remember myself later sitting in such a class, thinking about going to Tibet when I grew up.

I never heard Mom question her commitment to her mission. In an article for the church magazine *Gospel Messenger*, Mom described the children she sought to reach. "No one knows exactly how many little ones live in the valley, but everywhere along the road, in cornfields, darting behind cabuya plants, keeping watch over their tiny flocks of sheep—everywhere there are children. Each one stands as a challenge to us of the task to do." And she wrote about her frustration in trying to relate to the women of the community: "...too busy to attend meetings, too afraid of the priest's threats and too shy of foreigners. Language stands as a large barrier between her and the missionary, for her mother tongue is Quechua. And who can talk to her in another language of the things nearest her heart? So there is little or no progress we can report on work among the Indian women. Could you understand that just a smile and sincerely friendly greeting means a step forward for us, for we remember well that openly hostile stare and often a turned back when we approached. The field has hardly been touched. Everywhere these souls are waiting—not understanding what for—just waiting. God help us to bring them light."

She continued to work in missions and ministry throughout most of her life. But the same loneliness that is hinted at in her magazine article can be felt in her letters home, particularly when my father was away from home and she was left to care for four children. More than one started, "It's a lonesome Sunday night without our Daddy." Or, "Jeanne is playing the piano, Jan is doing homework and Becky and Bobby are bathing. Benton is gone again and we are lonely." Much later in life, when Mom faced death from cancer, my sister commented that it must be so lonely for her. She replied, "Oh, Jan, I have always been lonely." She once confided to my other, now-adult sister that she had sometimes wished that my father's car would go over an embankment or that one of the children would become seriously ill so that she would have a reason to return to her Papa in Indiana. It is hard, even now, for me to understand the deep desire she had to succeed as a missionary side by side with her own need for a home where she could feel security and belonging. I guess it means she was human.

Many years later, when I went as a newly graduated nurse to work in Brazil to test out my own inclinations to mission work, I learned how important it was to write letters to family "back home." Just as writing down these stories now connects me to my mother and my childhood home, writing allowed me to also savor memories of loved ones. As I would write letters, I pictured my parents reading them in their home in New Jersey. Writing seemed to create an invisible connection across the miles and the many new experiences. I have to believe that my mother felt that same connection with the family she so missed as she wrote her weekly letter "home."

My mother wrote her letters on a large Royal typewriter that sat on a metal typewriter table between the living room and dining room. The dining room had a large table and a buffet. On the wall behind the table hung an embroidered wall hanging of the Twenty-third Psalm, from which I memorized that scripture, the only one I have ever managed to memorize.

The Lord *is my shepherd; I shall not want.*
He maketh me to lie down in green pastures: he leadeth me beside the still waters.
He restoreth my soul: he leadeth me in the paths of righteousness for his name's sake.
Yea, though I walk through the valley of the shadow of death, I will fear no evil: for thou art with me; thy rod and thy staff they comfort me…

Our large living room had a fireplace on one end with a reproduction of Solomon's Head of Christ. A sunroom ran along the far side of the room, with a door out onto the porch. This door was rarely used, mostly if we had special guests whom we did not want to bring through the laundry room and kitchen. It was saved for formal occasions. Or, we kids might use it on a day like this, when life seemed more leisurely and my parents were the only adults in the house. Sundays were family time, and we used the living room for family times, for evenings around the record player with popcorn and Coke. *"Thou preparest a table before me… My cup runneth over."* We had to wait until evening, when the electric generator was started, to listen to records. One I especially remember was about a little boy who traveled through South America with his burro. Although I am poor at memorizing numbers, I know the altitude of Quito from a song on that record that said, "And Quito, the capital sits up high, nine thousand feet way up in the sky, in Ecuador, in Ecuador." We grew popcorn on the farm and shelled it ourselves, the sharp, pointy kernels tearing at our fingers. The Coke was purchased in wooden cases from the Coca-Cola factory in Quito, where we could watch the bottles on the conveyer belt being filled with the sweet, brown liquid and sealed with bottle caps.

Sunday afternoons were when the missionary families allowed themselves to relax. Challenges and conflicts that may have arisen in their work during the past week were set aside, and they relaxed and played. *"He leadeth me beside the still waters. He restoreth my soul."* There were games of volleyball and horseshoes. If someone had been in Quito on Saturday, they might have brought back a chunk of ice from the beer factory. It was kept in a shady place behind our playhouse, covered with sawdust and a gunnysack until Sunday afternoon when the ice cream freezer came out. A sledgehammer was used to break up the ice in the gunnysack, and we all shared in cranking the handle of the freezer or sitting on the freezer to keep it from wobbling as the ice cream got firm. Then we also shared in eating the rich ice cream.

After supper we kids would watch in amazement as the adults clowned around, trying to act out magazine advertisements in a game of charades. Though we did not have access to U.S. radio or television, we did get magazines like *Time* and *Ladies Home Journal*. Even the most serious missionary had to let his hair down for this game. I remember the missionary agronomist, a quiet, thoughtful man, almost putting his back out trying to act out, "I dreamed I crashed the headlines in my Maidenform bra."

Before all that play, in the afternoon, my mother always wrote her letter home. I watched Mom's back as she fed two sheets of onionskin paper with a carbon paper sandwiched between into the roller. She used the carbon to be able to write to her family in Indiana and to my Dad's family in Illinois at the same time. The mechanics fascinated me as I watched her at the typewriter. In front of her, the black keys with white letters surrounded by metal each stood on small metal arms, and when a key was struck, the corresponding letter would pop up from the array of letters fanned out before the paper on the black rubber roller. At the same time, black ribbon lifted into place so that the letter would be imprinted on the paper and on the carbon paper, if the key were hit with enough force. "Dear folks…" her fingers would fly over the keys. At the end of a line, a small bell chimed and she slid the shuttle back to the right, turning the roller ahead one line.

We had such good letters from both of you today, including the good news that Dad Rhoades is home again from the hospital. We are so relieved to know that and do hope that you'll really take it slow now and be up and around really good to go fishing with your son and grandson before too terribly long. Also we'll be thinking about you tomorrow and wishing we could all eat some of your cake with you—hope you can eat cake. And in case you can't blow out candles, my, how Becky and Bobby would love to help you.

We finally got the OK to go ahead and get the pick-up truck. All I hope is that nothing serious happens before we do. Last night we took a group into Quito to special meetings. I drove since we went in the old pick-up and the fellows said we women should sit in front. On the hill we saw the remains of a wreck in the afternoon. Matilde recognized the truck as that of her brother-in-law so we stopped and found that the brakes failed and he ran against the bank to avoid going over the hill, two killed and eight hospitalized. Just a bit after that as I went to slow down going around a curve, I discovered we had no brakes. We made the turn but I stopped and Benton drove on into Quito with low gear and emergency brake…"Yea, though I walk through the valley of the shadow of death, I will fear no evil: for thou art with me."

Bobby has been having pretty constant sore throat so we took him to the doctor yesterday morning. Dr. Roberts is in the states for a month but another doctor looked at him and said he'll have to have his tonsils out as soon as Roberts gets back…

We have been hauling every drop of water now for over a month. Every afternoon it clouds up and looks like it will let loose and pour but it just passing over us. Surely it will soon. George [another missionary] is kept busy just hauling water, and patching tires....

School started off with a bang this year. There are now eighty enrolled and 27 or so are first graders... Last Sunday was especially wonderful here. Eight people were baptized... We had a church dinner and a good social time afterward. Oh, we observed World Wide Communion Sunday too and had it after the baptisms... On Thursday I had to speak again at the women's meeting and I spent a lot of time getting prepared for that...

Other than Bobby we're all well, thinking of you often and praying for your health and well-being.

Love, Ruby

Even with airmail it took as much as two weeks for a letter to arrive and another two weeks to get a response. Mail was dropped off and picked up only when one of the missionaries got into Quito to the post office, where all the mail for the mission was put into the mailbox, Casilla 455, about in the middle of the long wall of mailboxes in the big echo-ey post office.

Letters were especially important to Mom. When she was six years old, her mother died from toxemia during pregnancy, leaving her motherless at the start of the Depression. Single fatherhood was not imaginable in those days, especially if you were desperately poor. My grandfather said in his memoir, "The Depression was on. Nobody had any money, or if they did, they were afraid to spend it." So, he placed my mother in the care of a childless couple who had expressed an interest in adopting her. Mom recalled him taking her to a church social where the couple was to pick her up, and when her father had to leave before the couple arrived, he left her sitting beside the road with her suitcase, waiting to be taken home by strangers. Grandpa thought having her with this couple was a good arrangement because "they attended church at Appleton, and she would sit with me at church."

Mom kept contact with the woman well into adulthood. After her death I found a Christmas card she had made for the woman while we were in Ecuador. But near her death from cancer, my mother confided to my sister that the man had molested her. The man and woman owned a general store, and my mother was sent over to help out in the store. There, among the shelves of supplies, the man fondled her so much that his dirty hands left stains on her dresses over her chest. He said, "Your brothers touch you like this, don't they?" Of course, little children cuddled and bathed together. So, she agreed. Finally, she told her father, who went to confront the man. The man said, "Her brothers have done no less." My mother told my sister that her father immediately removed her from that home and brought her and her brother to live with him in the tiny groundskeeper's cottage at the cemetery where her mother was buried.

In my grandfather's memoirs, which I found among the old family photos and letters, he says nothing about this episode. He recalls time spent with this family this way: "[He] took a notion to make a rock garden in his back yard, and I helped him gather all kinds of unique stones on the desert... We planted it with all kinds of flowers. My life with these big-hearted people is a pleasant memory." It was not a pleasant memory for my mother.

Through all of my mother's time away from her father in this sometimes frightening home, letters from her "Papa" kept her going. He would tell her little jokes and stories that he knew would be fun for a little girl. Sometimes he wrote backwards, a sort of code that required her to hold the letters up to a mirror to read them. He had become expert at reading upside down and right to left from proofreading the galleys of the newspaper he owned and published before losing it to the Depression. In his memoir, Grandpa said, "I learned to pick type from the cases and to replace it after using it with a fair degree of speed. Tearing down a piece of hand-set type was as big a job as setting it up... My main job was proof reading. I got so I could read it directly from the galleys of type. This meant reading upside down and from right to left." For almost six years of her life, until her father was able to move with his two youngest children to Indiana and start a successful printing business, letters from her papa were her lifeline. Now, missing him so much, the Sunday ritual of writing letters again connected them.

Sundays were also the day Mom made candy, just as she had learned to do from her mother-in-law, my paternal grandmother, who later helped me put on my "Freshman 15" with care packages of homemade candy. Sometimes, there was light, fluffy divinity made from the whites of our chickens' eggs. Better yet were the caramels. The Heifer Project Brown Swiss cows provided milk rich in cream, which rose to the top of the jars where it could be skimmed off for whipping cream, butter, or caramels. Mom stood by the woodstove stirring the syrup as the warm kitchen filled with the sweetness of caramel. When the syrup "sheeted" off the spoon, a few drops were dropped into cold water to test for its stage. Then the ball was fished from the water and dropped into one of our waiting mouths. When it reached the "soft-ball stage," the candy was poured into a buttered square metal pan to cool while Mom cut small squares of waxed paper with a serrated knife. When the caramels were cool enough, they were cut with a buttered knife into little squares to be wrapped in the waxed paper. Or, if we could talk her into it, we got a whole strip to hold in our hands and lick into sweet, sticky points as we went outside to play.

Years later, I learned that Mom wrote letters "home" and made candy on Sunday afternoons because she was homesick. While in Brazil, I would also feed the onionskin airmail paper into my little portable typewriter and start, "Dear folks… Things have been so up in the air around here that I sometimes feel hesitant to write to anyone. Now, I am finally learning to live with uncertainty so that it does not bother me quite so much and I am learning to enjoy life in spite of uncertainty…" In a letter to a college friend, I wrote, "My family seem to be doing fine and I miss them more than I can say. Jan is working at some kind of school for emotionally disturbed kids in Indiana… Becca was hospitalized, but it turned out to be mono. Fortunately, she has made a pretty speedy recovery and has already started to work again… It sounds like Mom is very busy and excited about some books she is working on. And Dad just got back from India and will be going again next month." And I might even make a batch of fudge or cookies to share with my fellow volunteers.

Letters home and something sweet from the kitchen.

Chapter 8
Kitchens Then and Now

I feel my excitement build on Saturday, my fourth day on this pilgrimage to rediscover my youthful self, as we drive along the road toward the Quebrada Grande, approaching the mission where I spent my childhood. Though the old farm no longer belongs to the mission, I have asked Mercedes to include this visit in my time in Llano Grande. From the road, I can see the windows of the sunroom at the end of the living room. The farm is now surrounded by a high wall and a locked gate. I have visualized every room since I have been back in Ecuador this time, but now we are actually going there. We pull to a stop just as a woman comes through the metal gate. Mercedes explains that we used to live here and the woman lets us in. Inside, we ask for permission to look around. The mission buildings now house elderly and disabled residents of the area, and the man in charge meets us on the porch of "our" old house, in a wheelchair. He tells us he was the first resident, and when we introduce ourselves, he invites us into the house to look around, in through the laundry room and down the hall past the bedrooms. What memories that brings back. I slept in each of these bedrooms.

The door to the kitchen is padlocked, and the man says it is now used just for storage. He says he recalls what a beautiful kitchen it was when he first moved in. His memories evoke my own, clearly, and I wish I could get inside to see the kitchen again. It was long and narrow, with windows on two sides, the black wood cookstove sitting along one wall over a floor of black and white tiles. Concrete countertops extended around the end of the kitchen to a sink on the opposite wall, under a small window, and a kerosene refrigerator sat beside the sink. The end of the kitchen had a large window overlooking the road from Cuatro Esquinas. The man tells us that he remembers wondering where the hot water came from if someone was cooking, until he finally realized that there was a hot water tank behind the stove in the wall. I tell him about getting back from trips all dusty and having to wait for the stove to heat up the water so we could take baths.

Mercedes leaves me alone. She wants to walk around the grounds. She and her husband Andrés lived in this same house for a while after the last missionaries left, so she probably has her own memories to recall. Standing there outside the kitchen door, running my hand along the wall, which now has a little peeling paint, I am wrapped in nostalgia. I recall the often-repeated story of the time my grandma, visiting and cooking at that stove, almost dumped sweet rolls onto the lap of the president of Ecuador. I may have been at school that day, but I feel like I was there for the whole thing.

Remembering Grandma in action in that Llano Grande kitchen also takes me back to that same grandmother's kitchen in Illinois. When we were on furlough from Ecuador, we always spent time at Grandpa and Grandma Rhoades's house, especially in their kitchen. We would stay there with my parents during family gatherings. Or my parents would leave us there while they made the rounds, speaking in the central Illinois churches that supported our mission.

After many years of living on rented farms, my father's parents had purchased a house in the town of Astoria, Illinois. Life had not always been easy for Grandpa. According to a family history compiled by my Aunt Nelda, "A sack of clover seed fell on Grandpa's back and severed spinal cord nerves. He was not a quitter; he studied diligently and passed the Real Estate Broker's Exam (though he had not graduated from high school). His love was helping young couples obtain loans so they could buy farms and stay in the community." He also sold insurance from the desk in his living room.

My grandmother just kept on cooking, often as if she expected a whole "thrashing" team for lunch. The kitchen was the heart of their two-story home, custom-made to accommodate Grandma's short stature. From my perspective as a seven-year-old, Grandma seemed to be about as wide as she was tall and was always wearing a pinafore apron. My aunts and uncles laughed about how on hot days out in the country, Grandma used to work with nothing on but the apron. "That time the pastor came calling: she backed up against the curtains to hide her bare behind," one would say.

"And, remember the time she fell down the stairs?" another put in. "Bud [my dad] ran over to her and turned her neck back and forth to see if it was broken. Then we had to figure out how to get some clothes on her before the doctor came."

My mother recalled her shock on her first visit to Dad's family. She had grown up with a father who was rather straight-laced. After the Depression, my mother, her brother, and their widowed father had moved from the cemetery caretaker's house in Colorado to Indiana, where he was able to start a business printing standardized tests for schools. When Mom was fifteen, her father remarried. His new wife had been a nursing instructor and never seemed fully comfortable in her role as a housewife. Mom grew to appreciate, even love, this big-hearted woman who was always ready to nurse sick or dying people in her community. But her father and stepmom could be stern and strict. Dad's family, on the other hand, was loud and casual. On that first visit Mom witnessed Grandpa jokingly picking up Grandma and sitting her on the stove. Telling this story always brought on peals of laughter from Dad's family.

A Formica kitchen table with chrome legs sat in the middle of Grandma's kitchen. Along one wall, the stove sat beside the refrigerator, and over the refrigerator hung a clock in the shape of a gingham cat, whose eyes and tail went back and forth rhythmically to mark the ticking of the clock. Grandma was always up before anyone else making wonderful smells come from the kitchen. I remember waking up to the smell of frying bacon and ham, from the hams and sides of bacon hung curing in the basement back in the coal room. In the winter we watched the coal truck lower its chute through the trapdoor into that basement, depositing coal beside the huge furnace. Although we were not allowed near the furnace, the basement in winter always had the metallic smell of coal burning to heat the house.

The basement was also where the men cleaned fish after fishing trips. Grandpa especially loved to fish and taught us to love it, too.

Before starting out, Grandpa dug worms from the yard with an electric worm probe that sent shock waves into the ground, forcing the night crawlers to the surface. Then we picked them up and put them into empty coffee cans. With the can of worms and our fishing poles, we drove to the lake to fish. Grandpa and Grandma always knew the best lakes for catching fish.

We parked the car at the edge of a field and climbed through the barbed wire fence. I remember watching in amazement as Grandma, still in her apron and white tennis shoes, fishing pole in hand, ducked between the wires, never getting snagged or scratched. We sat by the lake under a tree in the summer heat. Bees and mosquitoes buzzed in our ears. But if we tried to talk, we were shushed. "Don't want to scare the fish." My sister Jan was very patient and always caught the biggest fish, while I, on the other hand, watched the birds and the frogs plopping into the lake while pretending to also like fishing. Dad loved to fish, and I always wanted to be like him; but somehow, I was not able to develop the same love of fishing. Most of the fish were little bluegills and crappies, "Chips," Grandma called them.

Back at the house, while the men scaled and gutted the fish, my aunts started a fire in the backyard fireplace. Grandma seasoned cornmeal and put lard into a big kettle over the fire. The fish were then dredged in the cornmeal and fried in the hot grease as the picnic table was set. We had the fish with potato salad, sweet pickles, and pickled beets with hard-boiled eggs, pink from the beet juice. Then the watermelon was brought out and sliced. Grandma got out plastic aprons and tied them around our necks to catch the juice as we burrowed our faces into the sweet watermelon flesh and spit the black seeds on the grass.

Grandma made her own noodles. I have tried to learn to make a lot of things from scratch, but I do not plan to ever make noodles from scratch. I'm afraid that if I learn I will always feel like I have to make homemade noodles for Christmas and Thanksgiving dinners. Grandma mixed the eggs and flour and kneaded them together, and then she rolled out the dough very thin with a rolling pin. The sheets of dough were spread on dish towels on the picnic table behind the house. After those dough sheets had dried sufficiently, she rolled them up jelly-roll style and carefully sliced them into thin egg noodles. She cooked them in broth from the chickens that she had killed and dressed, so there were often little partially formed eggs from the cavities of the hens floating in the broth. These were a special treat, hidden in the fluffy yellow noodles.

Given the choice I would always choose to stay at my grandparents' house over going along with my parents to visit churches, as they did during furloughs. I remember sitting at the Formica table, watching the eyes of the cat clock going back and forth while Grandma made breakfast. There were always the eggs with the bacon and ham whose smell had awakened me, but my favorite was the fried mush. Grandma cooked cornmeal mush the day before and put it into loaf pans to cool in the refrigerator; then, in the morning, she sliced the mush and fried the slabs in hot bacon fat. It came out crispy on the outside with warm, soft centers. I floated my mush in more maple syrup than my grandsons, Seth and Michael, ever put on their pancakes in later days. Delicious!

As I sat at the table shelling peas or hulling strawberries, my aunts and other friends of Grandma's joined in the cooking and in the talk. The stories could fill a book. I imagined someday becoming a novelist and basing my stories on the stories I heard in that kitchen. My dad's oldest sister, Nelda, had gotten polio when she was one year old. In spite of paralysis of her right hand and foot, Aunt Nelda had attended college and worked as a medical laboratory technician. She seemed to know everyone in the small town of Astoria, although she had not lived there since finishing college. My dad's younger sister Marianne had come back to Astoria to work as a teacher after finishing college, and there she married a local boy who had always had a crush on her. As a teenager, I sometimes went with her to visit her husband's younger siblings in their farmhouses. They were not a lot older than I was but were already making homes for their young families.

Grandpa and Grandma's Illinois home was always open to guests. Aunt Marianne told me that when they lived on the farm, a church district executive often lodged with them. When he got into town, he would come to Grandma's kitchen door and say, "Orphy, put an extra tater in the pot." She could always make the meal stretch to feed one more.

My dad was considered something of a local celebrity, and our visits were chronicled in the local paper. Here's an earlier one, from his bachelor days:

> From the *Journal Star*, Peoria, Illinois, May 1941:
> Benton, the elder son, early interested in the farm, entered the 4-H and was president of his club two years. Following high school, he attended college and is president of the senior class of '42. His interest in speech has brought him honors in debate and oratory, representing his college in the state finals this year with his speech, "America in Us." Following this contest, he was elected to Tau Kappa Alpha, national fraternity of public speakers.
> Minister Since Youth
> He has been a minister since the age of 17. He is especially interested in the social and economic problems of our nation. In the summer of '39 he studied labor problems in the anthracite coal field of Pennsylvania. Last summer he was sent to study problems in Old Mexico. His chief interest is in finding ways to bind nations together with Christian democracy. With all his activities, he still loves to help out on the farm.

Sunday evenings, the Church of the Brethren pastor would often come for supper, with the traditional Sunday supper for guests in Grandma's kitchen always oyster stew. Oysters seem a strange tradition for a midwestern farm family, and likely they were not cheap. But they could be purchased at small groceries in Peoria, perhaps coming by train from Baltimore or up the Mississippi and the Illinois Rivers from the Gulf of Mexico. I remember Grandma cooking the potatoes and milk in a large pot on the stove. The briny oysters came in a cardboard carton that she opened and poured into the pot. The pastor and his family, along with the rest of us, all nodded in agreement as we sprinkled oyster crackers on the stew. "Orphy, you do make the best oyster stew in all of Fulton County."

You didn't have to be a pastor, church executive, or even a blood relative to be invited into the home and family; others also were welcomed. When Aunt Marianne was about ten years old, one of her jobs was to lead the hay horse back and forth beside the barn, operating the pulley that lifted hay up into the barn loft. When she got tired of doing this, her father went to the man down the road and asked if this man's son Harry, just a little younger than Aunt Marianne, could come and help with the horse. Grandpa saw more reason to do this than just having another hand with the hay, because the neighbor had experienced a number of personal tragedies, including the loss of his wife and an older son. Grandpa seemed to know that Harry needed more than what his father could offer him. Harry spent the whole summer with them. When it was time to go back home for the start of school, Grandma found Harry crying on the swing when she went to call him for dinner. "I don't want to go home. I want to stay here with you," he said. Harry moved in and grew up as a brother to Marianne.

When my father was studying at the seminary in Chicago, he noticed a boy sleeping under the elevated train platform: he brought the boy to his apartment and fed him. Then, he checked with the police and learned that Eddy had a habit of running away. The police were planning to send him to reform school the next time they picked him up. Dad brought Eddy home to Astoria. Eddy was not an easy guest; Aunt Marianne said that he once killed some of Grandma's chickens and left a note telling her he had done it. Still, he continued to come to Astoria during the summers. I remember him teasing me and my sister, tying knots in our jump ropes and coloring the pictures in our coloring books. Yet, it seemed that he was always welcome in my grandparents' home.

Aunt Marianne recently said about Grandpa and Grandma, "They didn't see a lot of the world, but the world came to their door." A German exchange student spent her senior year of high school in their home. Roma had lost her father and brothers in World War II. She came home from school crying when they got to the part of U.S. history about the war, so Grandpa went into the school and arranged for her to be excused when the class studied World War II. Roma continued to correspond with Grandpa and Grandma as long as I can remember.

I look up from my reveries to wonder what is taking Mercedes so long out there on the grounds of this old home of mine. Still, it is pleasant to stand here, nobody around and no responsibilities, and remember these wonderful and colorful people who were my dad's parents. They came to this very house to visit, and it was one of the only long trips they took away from Astoria, to visit my family in Ecuador at Christmas in 1951. This is how the famous rolls-on-the-kitchen-floor story began. Grandpa and Grandma arrived at the airport in Quito, and we brought them home to our house in Llano Grande. After adjusting to an altitude that can make one feel exhausted, they made themselves at home in our little farming community. Perhaps it felt familiar to them after their many years as tenant farmers. Grandma talked non-stop to Maria, the young woman who helped Mom with housework, though Maria did not understand a word of English. Grandpa would go out walking on his own. When he came back he told us about the farming methods of the neighbor man with whom he had conversed while the man plowed his field with the single-blade plow pulled by a pair of oxen. We were amazed at how much they were able to learn without speaking a word of Spanish. A loving and open spirit takes one far in promoting goodwill and understanding.

While in Ecuador, Grandma, whose cakes, pies and breads were always first to sell at bake sales "up town" in Astoria, had the opportunity to bake for the president of Ecuador. The president at that time was the progressive Galo Plaza Lasso. His family owned many dairy farms throughout the mountains of Ecuador. Dad had met him at the annual fair in Quito where cattlemen exhibited their livestock and where the offspring of the Heifer Project Brown Swiss cattle always competed well. Galo Plaza was also interested in the school and the medical work that were being done at the mission, and he planned to replicate it for the tenants who lived on one of his haciendas, so he came to visit the mission early one morning.

As President Plaza and his bodyguards walked around the farm with my father and grandfather, Grandma was busy making breakfast in the kitchen. I imagine that she knew her sweet roll recipe by heart. It is the same recipe I still use at holidays, after she gave it to me in a box of her recipes the year I got married. The box of recipes started with a little poem. "We may live without poetry, music and art; we may live without conscience and live without heart; we may live without friends; we may live without books; but civilized men cannot live without cooks…Some of my favorite recipes."

I am now imagining what is behind that locked kitchen door, peeking in my mind through the doorway to the now-empty kitchen. I recall with love particularly that big, black wood cookstove that sat along the wall, which provided our home with both good meals and hot water. Baking in the oven of the woodstove would not have been a problem for Grandma. She was experienced at judging the difference between a "medium oven" and a "hot" one and had probably used a woodstove early in her marriage. The altitude, though, was a new challenge for her.

"You need to be careful," Mom would have told her. "Things rise quickly here and then they fall. We always need to tip-toe around the kitchen when there is a cake in the oven." Even with great care, cakes usually came out stadium-shaped.

I smile as I think about that day when the president visited this home, our home. Grandma's hands were up to the challenge. She could feel when the bread dough was smooth and elastic and judge when to punch it down after the first rising if it rose too quickly. She warmed up the milk, melting the butter in it, then added the sugar, salt, and dry yeast. Then she kneaded in the right amount of flour. Granulated brown sugar was not available for filling the spirals of dough. Maria, our helper, had to help grate brown sugar off the solid cake of raspadura, the raw sugar Mom had brought from the market.

The rolls were light and syrupy with pecans Grandma had brought from the States for our Christmas baking. The president and his entourage were seated around the dining room table for breakfast. Grandma took the rolls from the oven and inverted them onto a plate. Then, as she started into the dining room, she tripped and fell. She would always recount saving the sweet rolls from hitting the floor and being able to serve them to the president of Ecuador. He never knew how close he came to not getting to share in the amazing bounty from Grandma's kitchen.

The story of Grandma baking for the president of Ecuador was often repeated around the Formica-topped kitchen table in Astoria. Everyone would gasp as she told about dropping the sweet rolls.

Her face would light up, and she would beam while modestly nodding when my aunts would say she should feel so honored to have baked for the president and to have sat beside him for breakfast that day. But he was the one who should have felt most honored to have been able to enjoy the baking from Grandma's kitchen.

The man who has been showing me around has returned, and I move away from that locked kitchen and onto the front porch where Mercedes is waiting. "This is the house where I brought my first two babies after they were born," she says. "And it is where we shared such happy times as children. Things change, but time can't change the happiness we shared here, can it, *amiga?*"

Together we walk to the truck where her daughter Elizabeth is waiting. I feel somewhat possessive of this, my childhood home. But I realize that Mercedes (and Elizabeth) carry memories of an early childhood spent playing on this very porch and front yard.

Chapter 9
HCJB

There was a time, after we had first arrived in Ecuador and I was a very little girl, when I did not know these grandparents or any of my family back home. I only knew the community where we lived, day to day. It was my world. To bridge that gap between mission field and the comforts of family in the United States, there was local missionary radio, HCJB.

I was reminded of the presence of this radio station when I first arrived on this current trip to Ecuador. Coming into Quito with the medical brigade, before I came out to Mercedes's family and Llano Grande, we were landing at the new airport. I learned that the airport is located in Pifo, now a suburb of Quito, and I realized it must have been necessary to tear down the transmission towers of our missionary HCJB radio station to build the new, state-of-the-art terminal and landing strips. HCJB now focuses on getting portable solar-powered radios into the hands of local people around the world and on supporting partner radio stations in indigenous communities to provide Christian programming to their own communities. But I remember when HCJB was the radio station heard around the world and played a role in my childhood.

Looming over all my memories of Quito are those transmission towers of the Christian radio station—Heralding Christ Jesus' Blessings, Voice of the Andes, Voz de los Andes, or VozAndes, as the local people still call it. The school I attended through eighth grade stood right next to the station, so close, in fact, that a fan in one of the classrooms sometimes picked up programs. Imagine hearing hymns being sung from a whirring fan!

Ecuador is located on the equator, the middle of the earth. Through the country run the Andes Mountains, the longest exposed mountain range in the world, with their height only surpassed by the Himalayan range in Asia. Mount Chimborazo in Ecuador forms the point on the earth's surface that is most distant from its center. That height made it an ideal location for shortwave radio transmission. Unlike AM and FM radio, shortwave transmissions bounce off the ionosphere, making it possible to transmit over long distances, even around the earth.

In order to extend its reach even further, the station also had towers in the high mountain village of Pifo. I once spent a weekend in Pifo with one of my classmates whose father was a technician at the transmission station. Above the tree line the landscape was barren with dry grass and little more: even cactus did not grow well there. Wind whipped around the small, flat-roofed houses in the mission compound, and acres of transmission towers with wires and cables going in every direction loomed against the backdrop of the spectacular snow-capped mountains. My friend had a horse that she rode bareback through the grass, careful to avoid tripping over the many cables that steadied the tall towers. The site is so windy that when the city of Quito built their new airport in Pifo in 2009, it became necessary to schedule landings and takeoffs of large international aircraft at night when there is less wind.

The station's programs were heard virtually anywhere in the world. Since the programming was live, Christian preachers and musicians broadcasting from the station spoke languages of most parts of the globe, particularly from Eastern Europe and the newly formed Soviet Union. The missionaries at the station took special pride that their programs brought the gospel to people in those "Godless countries behind the Iron Curtain."

The radio station also provided a service for nearby missionaries. On the first Monday evening of each month, HCJB hosted "Back Home Hour." This was a time when missionaries and their families could come to the station and send messages to their families by shortwave radio, a chance to share news with family far away, wherever far away might be. And we were there, ready to talk.

Living at the middle of the earth, without Skype, email, or cell phones, as I've said, we had to depend on airmail letters that took up to two weeks to arrive. In a crisis, one could send a telegram. Or, if you knew someone with a ham radio, it might be possible to actually have a two-way conversation. For general voice communication, though, we relied on the shortwave radio broadcast. The first Monday of the month, we hurried through supper. Washed and combed, we crowded together in the cab of the green International pickup truck in our pajamas so that we could be carried right into bed if we fell asleep on the way home. As we wound our way up the hairpin curves of the rough Pan-American Highway into Quito, we rehearsed what we were going to tell Grandpa and Grandma, people I could not at that young time in my life even picture. "We have a new kitten… I learned to walk on stilts…I have a loose tooth."

At the radio station, we waited on chairs in the hallway outside the studio. Then it was our turn. The walls of the studio were covered in cream-colored acoustic tiles with rows of little holes to absorb sound. Several clocks in the wall showed the time in Quito, London, Moscow, and other cities, and a thick glass window separated the studio from the control room, where huge reels of audiotapes were mounted on machines with tiny lights and knobs. The light fixtures were shiny metal discs that had once been records.

Inside the studio two or three radio microphones stood on stands with cords extending from them across the floor. Suspended, as if from cranes, the mics hung from metal bars that balanced on the upright support. These odd mechanical things looked like angular metal boxes covered with a fine wire mesh. The assistant would pull one of the chairs that sat along the wall over to the mic so that we children could reach it, but we were not to touch that mic. It was hard for my little legs to balance on the chair but not grab the mic for balance.

One Monday, when it was finally my turn, I completely forgot what I was going to say. The thing is, I actually believed the people we were talking to lived inside that microphone, and it was an odd, scary thing. As that small girl in a big studio, I imagined that the mesh holes around the mic allowed whoever lived inside to breathe. "I guess the cat's got her tongue," my father joked, though I did not see any cats and felt my tongue in my mouth.

My mother prompted, "What did you want to say to Grandpa

and Grandma?" These may have been my mother's parents, her dad and stepmom, to whom we were speaking, or my dad's. At that time, I didn't really know either set of grandparents, so these people I was addressing were just an abstract idea. Inside that contraption.

I looked at the precariously suspended mic where I supposed they lived. "Our kitty had babies," I blurted out. Then I backed off the chair. On the way home, I asked my parents, "Do Grandpa and Grandma have legs? What do they eat?" I was still trying to figure out how they could really fit into that little microphone. Not understanding why I asked that, my parents just laughed.

Later that year, I learned who that Grandpa and Grandma really were. Shivering on the tarmac of Midway Airport in Chicago, still nauseated from the bumpy plane ride, I staggered down the stairs into the darkness and cold. Hands reached out to me, tweaking my cheeks and pulling at my white-blond Tonette curls. "Jeannie, you have grown so much. Last time I saw you, you were just a little baby." Who were all of these strangers who seemed to think they knew me and that I should be glad to see them?

"Give Grandpa and Grandma a kiss," I was instructed. "Oh, look at how Alan and Marilyn have grown!" my mother exclaimed. When my mother was fifteen, as I've previously said, her father remarried, and the couple had two children. Alan and Marilyn were my mother's half-siblings, but they were closer in age to my sister and me. Alan was in third grade, and when we visited, he read the comics from the Sunday paper to us as we lay on the living room carpet.

From the Chicago airport, we were whisked off to these grandparents' ranch-style, Indiana limestone house, beside my grandfather's test printing business in northern Indiana. Unlike my dad's parents in Illinois, my maternal grandparents had wall-to-wall carpet on the floors and picture windows in both the living room and the dining room. I loved to lie on the window seat in the dining room with this grandma's huge calico cat and watch my mother's dad talking into the two-piece phone. He held the earpiece to his chest where his hearing aid receiver was located. The sweet aroma of his traditional wheat pudding caramelizing in the oven wafted from the kitchen.

After dinner, we joined my grandparents and my aunt and uncle in their living room to listen to the "Back Home Hour," direct from Ecuador. We were on the other end of these monthly transmissions now! Their shortwave radio was housed in a large wooden cabinet with ornately carved wood covering the brown fabric that protected the speaker, and as the radio warmed up, it began to emit high whistling sounds and sharp crackles as the shortwaves bounced off the ionosphere. My uncle gently nudged the knob that adjusted the dial behind the little plastic window and readjusted the wires at the back of the radio. With the slight movements, we could occasionally make out a human voice talking through the static.

"This is HJCB (muffled sounds, crackle) …elcome to (high pitched whistle) …ome hour." (More sharp crackles) Then I heard a child-like voice. "Hi, Gran… (whistle, crackle) …is Lois."

"It's Lois," Mom said to me. "Remember her from the nursery school at the radio station?" I wasn't sure that I did. But I nodded and pretended to be interested.

"Our turtle (muffled sounds, high pitched whistle) nursery school. (crackle, squeak)…lost."

That did interest me. Mom and Dad sometimes dropped us off at the nursery school while they ran errands in Quito. The one-room nursery school building had a pet box turtle who was an escape artist. It sounded to me like he had made it out again. Through more squeaks, crackles, and whistling, adult voices could be heard. They reported on their work with native people. They communicated their travel plans for furlough trips. I soon lost interest and drifted away.

In spite of the spotty reception in the early days, the radio station managed to reach people throughout the world. Using the material from used records, an engineer devised inexpensive, simple transistor radios that could be found in the thatched-roof huts in my home community. Sometimes we would walk up to a house to hear hymns being sung or preaching from the radio as families gathered on their porch to listen. Their voices also reached countries around the world and the station sometimes received messages from people in the Soviet Union thanking them for their programming. This instrument was effective in spreading the gospel, but just as importantly to us, it also served as a means for families to keep connected over the many miles.

President Galo Plaza of Ecuador at breakfast at our mission. To his right in the photo is my grandmother, who was serving her famous carmel rolls for this important occasion. He was considered to be modern minded.

My father Benton, Felda Hochstedler, Roland Flory, Ruby, and two others from the mission playing charades at one of our Sunday night recreation parties. Felda was a fellow missionary and Roland was a trained agronomist who lived, with his family, on our mission grounds.

Dear Grandma Sellers,

It certainly doesn't seem possible that another Christmas season is here. The weather here in Quito never changes, except to rain, and the days are so warm and sunshiny. The girls play outside all morning without sweaters.

Besides being busy getting ready for Christmas, we're making plans to move at last to our home in Calderón. The house isn't done yet, but we've built a large garage with extra space for storage and we plan to move there. We still are without water and will have to haul all we use. But it's so expensive living here in Quito and besides, we find nothing progresses when Benton isn't at the farm. We've had a difficult time this past year learning that mañana (tomorrow) may mean any day in the next several months. But I'm sure we've learned a lot about our friends here and all will go easier now. We are looking forward now to the coming of the Claude Wolfe family to help us in the work here.

Our two girls are growing so fast. Jeanne speaks Spanish quite well now and often mixes the two languages. They are happy little ones and sure cheer the days for me.

We appreciated so much the birthday gift money that the Fostoria church sent to us. I hope they got my letter of thanks.

We are looking forward to visiting you just a bit over a year from now. Please give my love to Aunt Fannie and her family. I think of you all many times. Love, Ruby

A Christmas letter to Grandma Sellers from my mother shows our yearning to be in touch..

SPRINGS IN THE DESERT

Patience will oftentimes reveal hidden springs of spiritual growth

No wells in the Calderon Valley; so the mission has to depend on the cistern and the water tank

J. Benton Rhoades
Bella Vista, Ecuador

CALDERON has no well water. On various occasions wells have been drilled here to depths around three hundred feet, but all dry holes. Some say that the valley was formed by a river of volcanic lava which subterranean water could not possibly penetrate.

"So," said a learned Ecuadorian teacher and lawyer, "it is hopeless to try to strike water there. As hopeless," he continued, "as to try to propagate a faith like Christianity among its thousands of Indians whose mentality is the mentality of a beast of burden."

I have thought often of those words. For the story of evangelism in Calderón these past three years has not been one of success but one of faith — of drilling. True the thought life of the Indian seldom if ever transcends the realm of corn, mud bricks, burros, work and drink. The world of abstract ideals is not their world. They do not, like the Greeks of Paul's day, sit in the public plaza waiting to hear some new thing. Even when a few of them do gather together on Sunday, preaching is not easy. Many times the preacher finishes his evangelistic message with the disheartening fear that he has just drilled another dry hole—that his message has failed to reach the soul of the Indian though the people sat in an orderly fashion and listened with seeming good attention. At such times one would despair of the task except for faith in God, who goes on speaking directly to men's hearts when the preacher has failed.

Then there are other occasions when one feels that the spoken message takes on life and strikes a responsive chord in the life of the Indian. The evangelist asks a young Indian farm hand to harvest a patch of potatoes while he is to be out on visitation. The young Indian refuses, saying, "But, señor, it is not good to dig potatoes when you are away. Do you not know that one always steals potatoes when one digs potatoes, even if the owner of the field is watching as carefully as he can? It is unheard of that one should be asked to dig potatoes when the boss is not even present. I cannot." Then the potato field becomes the church where two in quiet conversation come face to face with Christ, who was tempted in every way even as we and has now promised never to leave us alone in our temptations if we belong to him. The occasion has the character of true worship. The missionary goes on his journey. The potatoes are dug and a child of God has experienced for his first time the joy of walking in the presence of the Unseen, who is nearer to us than hands and feet.

Another day the missionary has offered to take a young Indian girl to the hospital for a hip X ray. Suffering great pain

14 GOSPEL MESSENGER

This magazine article was published in The Gospel Messenger *August 25, 1951.*

and unable to walk she is at last willing to have the difficulty diagnosed. At the hospital the findings are not hopeful. On returning home at evening the missionary must break the news to the family that tuberculosis of the bone has eaten away most of the ball-and-socket joint—tissue that will not replace itself. Maybe streptomycin and good food, maybe nothing short of a miracle of God will arrest the infection and stop the damage from spreading to other parts of the body. She will doubtless remain a cripple for life. The missionary, as the link between the Indian and the world of medicine, finds it his hard task to relay that report. But, as he stands there in the dusk with this family, he senses the presence of One beside him who says, "Now is the time to tell them that I will be their strength and comfort. If they will be my people, I will be their God." The message is given. The patio of an Indian hut becomes the church and God becomes real to an Indian family.

It is the afternoon of Easter. A young father comes staggering down the road from the drunken feast that characterizes the resurrection day in this country. Beside him walks the mother still sober enough to carry on her back their year-old son. The evangelist, seeing that the father recognizes him, steps near enough to say, "I'm sorry, Jose, to see you this way today. God must be sorry too." Then comes the usual excuse, that friends had invited, in fact obligated him, to take just one cup of *chicha* in honor of the day and that surely there was something wrong with that *chicha*. Next afternoon Jose passes by the mission farm to say that something has been worrying him all night and all day. Before time comes to sleep again he wants to talk with the missionary to say he is sorry for the way he looked yesterday. The prayed-for moment has come when one Indian is willing to hear the voice of God about the body being the temple of the Spirit, the sins of fathers being visited upon their children, and about the health and joy within the Christian home. He goes away refreshed, thinking for the first time about the nobility of life that God has reserved for man and of the promise of the risen Lord that, through him, the good can conquer all the evil that is in us.

All year in the canyon that borders the Calderón Valley there are little trickles of water issuing from the stone. So doubtless deep down under the earth there are tiny currents if one could only find them. Just so within the lives and souls of these people there is somewhere, even after centuries of peonage and false teaching, a current of spiritual sensitivity. That current, if tapped even in one person, may spring forth into a stream of living water, blessing not only that one life but the lives of his neighbors who come to drink thereat. This is our faith. Hence, we go on drilling.

Centuries of peonage and of being regarded as little better than beasts of burden as well as the fear of the church make the Indians slow to respond

Living as Neighbors
Continued from page 13

the approval of the police court, Pedro was paroled to our mission for three months. He worked eight hours each day without pay for those three months. Since his family lives very close, he could go home for all his meals. He reported each evening at seven o'clock and slept in a *choso* (a small grass-roofed hut that is used by people who sleep outside to guard their animals). He did not stay to guard our animals. He stayed at our request, so that the community would know where he was in case other robberies were committed.

Our other neighbors had varied reactions to such a strange way of handling a robber. They were sure we were crazy and would repent of such a decision. They said that Pedro was laughing up his sleeve because we were so naive as to treat him kindly.

Pedro completed his three months without one complaint or act of resentment. And now with the repair work going on in the school building, he has been hired and has been faithful in his work.

Of course, we do not know what the outcome will be. He may attempt to rob our home again. But after spending eight months in jail, he might have tried again anyhow. We are sure of one thing. Our neighbors have seen someone handled in a Christian manner. They had never known of such treatment before. We hope it will develop the feeling of neighborliness and that the people will come to realize that there is something different about the foreigners who have moved into their community. Maybe it is that strange religion they profess.

Turn to page 23 for Plans for Permanent Work in Ecuador, by Leland S. Brubaker

Mom Ruby Rhoades, Jan, and Jeanne at Grandma and Grandpa Rhodes' house in Illinois. We are all enjoying watermelon.

Benton, Jan, Ruby, and Jeanne reading at Christmas time.

Benton Rhoades showing Ecuador's President Plaza the farm's expanding argricultural mission to the country.

Chapter 10
Piano Virtuoso

It is Sunday morning now in Llano Grande, my fifth day here. I slip into one of the wooden pews of the Iglésia El Mesías, The Messiah Church, nestled in a small grove of eucalyptus trees. Though I am aware of this congregation, the building in this location was built after we left Llano Grande. Both sides of the church have panoramic windows, looking out at the trees. Wooden beams support the corrugated roof. Someone brings a bunch of long-stemmed red roses and places them in a clay pot in front of the podium. Fresh flowers are now one of Ecuador's major exports, and they are readily available throughout the village. A computer projects a welcome onto the wall in front. I am wearing a poncho; it is cooler here than I had remembered.

A praise song pops onto the wall from the computer as the song leader and praise ensemble move to the stage. The song leader is Mercedes's oldest son German, and her daughters and granddaughters are in the ensemble. After a few choruses, the Sunday school classes take turns filing to the front and sharing what they have just learned. Parents step into the aisles to snap pictures. I do not feel intrusive snapping a few pictures myself.

Following the reading of the scripture from Jeremiah 18, I am invited up to give the message. I share greetings from my home church in Indiana and from the Church of the Brethren in the States. Then I speak of my own recent losses of my husband and son. "When I was feeling most desperate, a song from my childhood in this church came to me '*Has lo que quieras de mi Señor. Tu el alfarero, yo el barro soy.* Have Thine own way, Lord. You are the potter; I am the clay.' I realized that I am the clay in Jeremiah's story of the potter. I must yield in my Maker's hands."

I finish and sit down, still not really believing that I had just preached a whole sermon in Spanish. Mercedes's teenaged granddaughter Sisa slips in beside her grandmother and hands her an old hymnbook. "Can you find the song Jeanne mentioned?" Like so many churches in the States, the church has put away the hymnbooks and now sings songs projected on the wall. We page through the book and find the hymn. German lines it out while Sisa accompanies on the piano and the congregation sings the old, familiar hymn. I watch Sisa play, sightreading a song that was not familiar to her. She plays so well. I wonder where she learned and who taught her.

I remember when I was around five and started taking piano lessons. At that time, there were a lot of articles in the women's magazines about child prodigies. Liberace was only seven when he won a scholarship to the Wisconsin Conservatory of Music. Philippa Schuyler, who was hailed as a young American Mozart, gained national acclaim as a child prodigy on the piano, and her photo graced the covers of weekly newsmagazines and monthly women's magazines.

Mom read their stories; she may have seen in them a way to escape the monotony of her life as a missionary wife in the dry hills near Quito, Ecuador. I imagine that the same yearning to see new places that brought her to Ecuador now surfaced in her hopes to see the world with her child prodigy daughter. She told herself she would not be one of "those" mothers who pushed her child to the child's detriment, but she was also sure that I would be a child genius on the piano. This could be because I would get so frustrated practicing that I would sometimes hit my head on the piano and cry: artistic sensitivity, to her. That was all it took to convince Mom that I, like Liberace, had genius, passion. If only she could have seen that the passion was not for the music but for pleasing her.

Our piano was a small upright by Gulbranson that my parents brought from the States with them. The G in "Gulbranson" was right over the middle C, where it was easy for me to find and get my fingering. With both thumbs on middle C, my little fingers reached to the adjacent keys. The white ivory keys were smooth, the back of the piano too tall for me to see over. My legs hung over the edge of the piano bench, too short to touch the floor or those fascinating pedals.

There was a great supply of potential piano teachers since the HCJB radio station was in Quito and, at that time, much of the programming was live. Like Liberace's first piano teacher Florence Kelly, who taught him between programs at a radio station, so the story went, my teacher was a professional pianist who gave me lessons in the same studios where live Christian programs were produced. And, like Liberace's teacher, my first teacher was also "furiously uncompromising, willful and outspoken."

My teacher Janice Terwilliger (Aunt Jan), with her long blond hair primly braided and wrapped around her head, was strict and demanding. She had come to Ecuador from the United States in response to her missionary calling and spent most of her life working at the radio station. Only recently I learned that Aunt Jan grew up in Indiana, and after returning from Ecuador and until her death, she lived just twenty miles from where I now live. I would have loved to know she was so near and to reconnect with her as an adult, reconstructing my memories of a childhood in Ecuador. While I was taking lessons from her, those connections back in the States were irrelevant to a child whose home was Ecuador and to whom the States was just a place one visits when the family is on furlough.

Strict, she was. If a student hit the wrong note, she was likely to get rapped on the knuckles with the pencil Aunt Jan used to write assignments. I slowly worked my way through John Thompson's beginner book, learning to plink out scales and the tunes of "Papa Hayden's dead and gone, but his music lingers on" and "Good King Wenceslas looked out." Once a week, I would travel into Quito with whichever one of my parents had business or shopping to do. They would drop me off at the radio station, where I showed Aunt Jan what I had learned and got a new assignment for the coming week. When I boarded at the school next door, I just walked over to the station and sat down on the piano bench.

I remember sitting in our living room practicing the piano with

Mom beside me. The room always seemed large with its exposed wooden beams. The sofa under the beams was sprinkled with a fine, powdery wood residue from the termites in the beams; to my left was the sunroom with windows eternally coated with the road dust that billowed in whenever someone drove up the dirt road outside. Flies crawled around and buzzed at the windows.

Mom must have learned to play the piano when she was a child, though I never heard about that. I do know that she knew how to play and that the mission church had a small, portable pump organ that she played during services. To make it perform, the accompanist had to pump vigorously on pedals that worked bellows that forced air through reeds to make music. One of the other missionaries, Jim and John's mother, was so good at this that she could lead the singing while she pumped and played the accompaniment for the songs.

In front of me, sitting there at the piano, large, round notes floated across the pages along with pictures of young boys with powdered wigs and sleighs being pulled through the snow by prancing horses. My mother sat beside me in her apron and starched plaid cotton dress, putting her hands on mine to help me find the notes. Those hands were warm and soft, smelling of chopped onions from her cooking and Johnson's baby oil from changing my brother's diapers. It wasn't a passion for the music that kept me at the piano. It was the scent of onion and baby oil and my mother's undivided attention for this little part of her busy day, as she nurtured every aspect of her dream of my future piano accomplishments.

One day I was playing out in Dad's woodshop, which was also the garage for the electric generator, some tools, and general storage. The wood was what made it special. Fresh eucalyptus wood shavings fell from the plane Dad slid across the wood, and once he tasted a piece of the shavings, saying it was so he would know how the crib rails he was making would taste to Bobby when he chewed on them. We rustled through and kicked the fragrant shavings. There were several sizes of planes, but the really interesting one was the electric one. Even when the power was off, you could make it go around by turning the black rubber belt that connected it to the electric motor. When you pulled the belt, the shiny blades turned.

And then I stuck my fingers in! There seemed to be blood everywhere. I ran screaming into the house. "Oh, Jeannie, what have you done?" my mother cried as she cleared away the blood and inspected my fingers to see if any were missing. The power of her pain numbed any pain I may have been feeling. "Benton, how could you let the children play around those sharp tools? Weren't you even paying any attention?" She may have been crying for her child who was in pain, but I also suspected that she cried because she was sure that I had ruined my future as a child prodigy pianist by cutting off the tip of at least one finger. She was wrong on both counts. None of my fingers were permanently damaged. Not even scarred. But I was not destined to ever be an excellent pianist, just good enough to enjoy playing for my own relaxation.

In Ecuador, our piano recitals were always held in the studios of the radio station. Chairs were arranged on the risers used by chorale groups in broadcasting. We would dress up in our best clothes, and our parents watched from the chairs as each student took his or her turn at the grand piano in front of the studio. I am sure this helped my mother to picture me on a concert stage.

I did continue with piano lessons until junior high back in the States, when my friends and I rebelled against playing in recitals with little kids and quit the lessons. Our piano teacher held the recitals in the church basement, but by then, my friends and I felt that we were way too old to play in a recital with five-year-olds just learning to pick out a tune. We tried to negotiate with the teacher to let us host the punch and cookie table instead of playing in the recital, but no, playing in recitals was requisite for taking lessons with her. So we all quit.

My younger sister Becca became quite good at the piano, and she still plays well. I, on the other hand, worked only at playing show tunes, movie themes, and hymns for my own enjoyment and relaxation. I may not have become a Liberace nor even a Philippa Schuyler, but I am grateful that my parents made the effort to get me piano lessons.

When I was pregnant with my first baby, I purchased a used small, upright piano. We had saved money for my maternity care, but then I got a job with insurance coverage, so I had $500 that I could spend on a piano. The baby was now a week overdue, and I was getting very impatient. "It's a good thing the baby didn't come any later. Jeanne might have bankrupted us with her shopping," my husband would say. Trundling my very pregnant self up and down the streets of downtown Rockford, Illinois, on the hot autumn day, I went in and out of the various piano stores. Even the used pianos cost a lot more than I had to spend. I had no idea they cost so much. Then, at one store, the salesman told me they had just gotten in an old piano that was in the back being refurbished. We went back to look at it, and I knew this was the one. The price was right, but it also had a comfortable feel to it.

When my mother came after the baby was born, she walked into the house and exclaimed, "You got our old piano!" We were both confused because that piano was left behind in Ecuador twenty years before. That was when I realized that I had, in fact, gotten a Gulbranson just like we had in Ecuador. No wonder the piano felt so right to me! She pulled up a chair and sat down to play. I pulled a chair up beside her and watched her hands reaching out to the chords. This time, I listened as she played. And it was my hands that had the sweet scent of onions and baby oil.

Chapter 11
The Mayo Clinic

Our life was not always totally insular, confined to the mission community and occasional happy visits to relatives in the States. We had occasion to make longer visits of necessity, and not all of them were happy ones. One of the lowest times in my life happened at the same place where my own mother had also lived through one of her lowest, the Mayo Clinic.

Mom was there with my three-year-old sister Becca at Christmastime when Becca was diagnosed with an aggressive form of cancer and Mom needed to bring her "home" for surgery. I know that Mom wanted desperately to get back to the States, but not under these circumstances. As a young missionary mother in Ecuador, she had imagined one of her children getting sick and needing to come home, part of her ever-recurring homesickness. But now that it had really happened, it was not at all what she wanted. The happy singing of Christmas carols must have seemed to her to make a mockery of the grim stories behind the parents' faces she saw at Mayo. They must be asking, "How can the world go on, celebrating a joyful holiday when my world has just come crashing down around me? Where is the joy of anticipation when all that I anticipate is suffering and death?"

I was in second grade when Becca was diagnosed with vaginal cancer. It was the kind of cancer that young girls get if their mothers took DES (diethylstilbestrol) when they were pregnant. During the '40s and '50s, doctors prescribed DES to prevent miscarriages in women who had spotting during pregnancy. Sadly, when the daughters reached adolescence or young adulthood, many developed vaginal cancer, preventing them from ever bearing children and sometimes costing them their lives. Apparently, drinking milk from cows that were being given hormones had exposed Becca to DES in my mother's womb.

Becca had fallen off her tricycle and started bleeding from her vagina. My sister Jan, who was a year behind me in school, and I boarded at school during the week and came home on weekends. It was strange to see our little sister, who still used the potty chair, with a Kotex pad pinned into her panties.

The following week, we were practicing for the Christmas program at school when we were called to the principal's office. Mom and Dad were there with my little brother and sister. They said that Becca was very sick and needed to go to a hospital in the States and that they were on their way to the airport. Then they were gone. Jan and I did not really understand what all this meant, but we started to cry because we sensed that it was serious. Classmates stared and whispered. One little girl, though, offered to push us on the swing. We may have forgotten exactly who it was, but we would always remember her kind gesture.

> From Dad's memoirs:
>
> We were told that Becca should be at Mayo's in a matter of hours, but it was Christmas time and no airplane seats were available for love or money. Then there was a knock at the door. The one knocking was Bill McI, our travel agent friend. "I have news. The U.S. ambassador just now ordered a small navy plane based at Guayaquil to land in Quito at daybreak tomorrow to take Ruby and the two little ones to Panama. I've booked space on a commercial flight from there to Chicago."
>
> It was an answer to prayer. "Thanks Bill and thank God. We'll be there." We didn't sleep. There was planning to do. We had no idea how long Ruby would be away. How would we break the news to Jeanne and Jan who were eight and seven at boarding school in Quito? Should I plan to come later with them? I was in the midst of a legal hassle over land.
>
> In the wee hours, we wakened Becca and Bob, a babe in arms, to say they and Mother were going on a trip. Ruby was already packed.

> Now we got the little ones dressed and psyched up for travel. We loaded up the four of us in our used International pickup truck and drove over the three miles of dirt road and the twelve miles of cobblestone Pan-American Highway to the airport.
>
> We saw the sun come up over [the snow-capped mountain] Cotapaxi just as the small navy craft cleared the eleven thousand foot pass into the Quito valley. Ruby got on board and strapped Becca, pigtails flying, into the left seat behind the pilot. Ruby and Bob were buckled in behind the co-pilot and the engines started.
>
> What we didn't know when the plane taxied out on the grass runway was that the plane had loaded with gas the night before for takeoff at sea level, not at 9,000 feet altitude where the air is thin. I could see anxiety in the stance of the naval officer on the ground as the plane went to the very south end of the runway and began acceleration.
>
> At the north end of the air field stood a row of tall eucalyptus trees—no problem for the DC3s who took off there daily. As the pilot gained speed going north, the officer on the ground was more anxious. As the plane finally lifted off and began to climb, he called out, "God, damn. He'll never make it." But he did and they were on their way.

When Jan and I came home for the Christmas break from school, it was obvious that things were different. Of course Mom and Becca and Bob were not there, but it was more. Dad was lonely. He was sleeping on the bare mattress without sheets. He invited us to come and sleep in their big bed with him, so we did, but it felt strange to be in Mom and Dad's bed, and I only slept there because I knew Dad needed us. Dad tried to make it a good Christmas for us even without Mom. He cut a cedar tree and set it up in the usual place in the sunroom and got out the Christmas decorations. Weeping, he wrapped the little doll dresses that Mom had sewn from scraps of the dresses she had made for us and put them under the tree. Jan and I begged him to let us have the other missionary kids on the farm, Jim and John, come help us decorate the tree and make the Christmas cookies. He was too stressed to give us much resistance. As soon as he agreed, we regretted begging. I knew then how much he wanted to try to make it as much like it would have been with the whole family together.

In early February we joined Mom in the States. The flight to the U.S. had not been easy for her. She told us that Becca needed to pee and of course there were no bathrooms in the little plane, so the pilots had her pee in a little paper cup and threw it out over the ocean. Mom had to negotiate customs in Miami with a toddler and a very large eighteen-month-old who still refused to learn to walk. The airport in Miami was always hot and muggy, and the customs agents roughly opened all the luggage, rifled through it, and then left it for the traveler to repack and then make his or her connection. When Mom, Becca, and Bob arrived in Chicago, my dad's parents and siblings were waiting to take Bob home with them. My Aunt Marianne remembers Mom getting off the plane with the front of her blouse in shreds. Bob had clutched so frantically to her that he had torn up the bodice of the blouse. When Mom and Becca reached Minneapolis, Mayo had sent an ambulance to pick up this very sick child. When they saw a little girl with bouncing pigtails skipping off the plane, however, they turned around and left her at the airport. Mom had to find her own way to Rochester with her little daughter and locate a place to stay while she took Becca to her appointments.

Cancer treatment in the mid-50s had not nearly reached the point where it is now. At that time, the only real option was surgery, and the doctors did not think that would help with the aggressive cancer from which Becca was suffering. Mom spent that Christmas walking those cold halls alone, begging doctors to please help her little girl. The carolers, merrily singing "Jingle bells, jingle bells," must have seemed ironic in the face of her pain. Visiting hours even for parents were limited to two hours a day because "the children get so upset when their parents leave." Grandparents were not even allowed. When Mom's father came to visit, Mom broke into sobs. "Becca's grandpa has never seen her and he may never get a chance to see her. Please let him in." They let Grandpa look at her through a window in the door to the pediatric unit.

Mom poured her heart out in letters to Dad and took them down to the desk of the boardinghouse where she was staying to be mailed. After she finally got someone to operate on Becca and Becca was released from the hospital, the clerk at the desk handed

Mom all of the letters. "You did not put enough postage on them," he said. Meanwhile, Dad was frantic, awaiting some news of his wife and little girl. When airmail letters did not arrive, he even tried sending telegrams to ask what was happening. I found multiple messages in the Mission Board archives from Dad, trying to get news about Mom and Becca. When we got back to the States and when Mom was reunited with the family, Bob had learned to walk and just ignored Mom for abandoning him with strangers. She was, again, heartbroken.

Fifty-five years later, I walked the streets of Rochester, past the imposing, historic hospital. I ached to share this experience with my mother. She had walked these same streets alone, with Dad in another continent. I also walked them alone, without my husband, my primary source of support throughout the many years of our son Mike's illness. I shared in Mom's frustration and heartache across the years, and I yearned to connect with someone who really knew how it felt.

Just six months after my husband Mark died of leukemia, doctors told my son Mike and me that the inoperable tumor in his pelvis had become malignant. He had cancer. When we adopted Mike from Colombia at five years of age, we did not know that he carried the gene for neurofibromatosis, an inherited disease that causes people to grow tumors on nerves throughout their bodies. He had courageously lived with the effects of neurofibromatosis and endured more major surgeries than I was able to keep track of. I finally wrote down his whole medical history on my computer and, each time he had new complications, I printed the history and took it with us to the doctor.

Some doctors looked at the medical history, and others approached him as if they never had the information available. I was furious when one orthopedist we saw for complications from a previous spasticity surgery actually sent him for x-rays and then walked into the exam room and said, "So, tell me about how you injured your ankle. Was it a sports injury?" In addition to feeling that all my work was wasted, I was indignant that a medical professional would waste expensive medical resources doing unnecessary testing just because he was too lazy to look at the information provided by a patient before actually seeing him.

This current tumor filled Mike's pelvis, and the chief of surgery had not been able to remove it in an extensive operation that almost cost Mike his life when the doctor cut through an artery. I knew the outcome would not be good. But Mike wanted to do all he could. After all, he was only thirty-five years old and had really valued being able to live on his own, work, and drive a car, in spite of his increasing spasticity.

While Mike started on chemotherapy, I prepared my house to care for him as his disability worsened. I purchased a hospital bed on Craigslist as friends from church built a wheelchair ramp from the garage into the family room. I had a wheelchair lift installed on the back of my new car; fortunately, I had chosen a small SUV. And I abruptly, but necessarily, retired from my all-time favorite job as a pediatric nurse practitioner working with children with severe disabilities, leaving behind the job and the colleagues who had gotten me through my husband's long illness and death.

At the conclusion of several rounds of chemo, the oncologist recommended that we get a second opinion at Mayo Clinic. The clinic had experience doing a ghastly procedure called a hemipelvectomy, which involves removing half of the pelvis along with one leg. Pictures on the internet looked so awful that I had to quickly glance away. As a nurse, I had seen many difficult procedures and unusual wounds, but this procedure was more awful than anything I had ever imagined. Yet I gathered all the needed documents, sent them a detailed history, and prepared for the trip. For Mike, anything would be better than death, and what could I say? He wanted to cling to life with all his might, and if that's what he wanted, I would try to help him do it. I was his mother, after all.

Traveling with Mike would not be easy. He had lost bowel and bladder control, so there were boxes of Depends adult diapers. Just getting to and from the bathroom was challenging for him. Although a few rest stops had "family" restrooms, stops at McDonalds required me to go into the men's restroom to help him clean up and get back and forth between the wheelchair and toilet. While he went into the restroom, I waited outside. After a long wait, I called in to him. "Mike, do you need any help?" When he did not reply, I decided to go in. Holding my "diaper bag" up beside my eyes as I passed the men standing at urinals, I called out, "Woman coming through." Of course the handicapped stall was at the very back of the restroom. Although I tried to be matter-of-fact about cleaning him, I saw him wince as I leaned over to wipe him. I always referred to the adult diapers as briefs or pants, but he quite frankly called them diapers.

A plastic sheet would be needed to spare the bedding in the hotel, and we needed to find hotel rooms with shower chairs in the room and roll-in showers. He was on multiple medications for the pain, spasticity, and seizures. With the difficulty he had getting into a comfortable position in the car, he required frequent stops to stretch out tight muscles. At each stop I needed to lower the wheelchair lift on the back of the car, drive the motorized chair up to his door, and lift him out. Once when I was getting him back into the car, which I did by lifting and pivoting him as I had learned to do in beginning nursing, he snapped, "You don't have to throw me into the car like a sack of potatoes."

I said, "I'm sorry, but if I don't do it this way, I will hurt my back. Then you will have to go to a nursing home because I won't be able to take care of you." At one of our overnight stops, he said he wanted to ask me something. "Promise me that you won't ever put me in a home," he said with tears on his cheeks.

I wished I could promise, but I replied, "Mike, I'm sorry. I want to be able to keep you home and take care of you. But, with all that has happened to me in the last few years, I cannot make any promises about the future."

"I understand," he replied with resignation. His father's standard reply when I railed against the unfairness of his illness was, "It is what it is." Were we all learning the same resignation?

I had made a reservation at a hotel that looked like it was very close to the hospital so that we wouldn't have far to go to get to appointments. I didn't realize that most of Rochester is part of the clinic complex and that there is handicapped-accessible transportation to all of its various associated hospitals. This hotel was old and musty smelling, without a restaurant or any room service. If you wanted to order food, you called a local restaurant for carryout and they would deliver it to you. Mike loved Indian food, so that is what we ordered. Mike slept on the bed closest to the bathroom and I slept on a foldout sofa bed near the TV. It was easier for him to get to the bathroom, but I had to try to read over the noise of the action movies he liked to watch. On the plus side, when I apologized in Spanish to the Hispanic-looking housekeeper for the soiled bed sheets, she replied, "It's okay. I know that the people who come here come because they are very sick. Don't worry about the sheets." I wanted to hug her.

The first day at the clinic was disappointing. True to form, the neurosurgeon whom we saw first had not read anything I had sent him; he walked into the room and asked why we were there. I tried to ask if there was really anything they could do that would benefit Mike. He replied, defensively, "I am just getting to know his situation. I can't answer that." And he wanted to repeat all the scans we had done at home and brought for his review.

The final day, the doctors told us that surgery would be futile. The horrid surgery to remove a leg along with pelvic tissue was not an option. Each of the doctors wrote their reports, and the neurosurgeon referred to me as Mike's "caregiver." I suppose he didn't know that an adopted child is still your real child, not just someone you care for. Still, the oncologist's report noted that she was giving us the grim news on the one-year anniversary of Mike's father's death. When one goes through such a traumatic experience, you will never forget those people who touched you as a real human being.

So then we waited in our musty hotel room, away from all of our normal supports and activities. Mike didn't feel like getting out and seeing anything, and I grew tired of Indian takeout. On the weekend, we did do a little "shopping therapy," and he, very sweetly, encouraged me to buy a new dress. At the store, Mike got out of his wheelchair and rested on a love seat by the dressing rooms while I tried on the dress. When I came out I saw a security guard trying to wake him, but when the guard saw me speak to Mike, he left. Later, I questioned the clerk about why he had been called. "Oh, he was just making his routine rounds," she said. I suspected that a tired, sick-looking Hispanic young man resting on the love seat in a high-end women's clothing store had caused alarm. Didn't they know, like the housekeeper at the hotel, that the main reason people come to Rochester is because they are desperately ill?

I bought a novel and a watercolor paint set and small pad of watercolor paper, and I started a Caring Bridge site to keep in touch with family. But mostly, while Mike watched TV, I kept redialing the clinic to find out what was next. This went on for several days, requiring me to find a washer and dryer because I had only brought a few days' change of clothes. I used the hotel phone rather than my cell phone, thinking it was more economical since we were across the street from the hospital. Surprise! At the end of the stay, I found that the hotel had charged me seventy-five cents for each time I hit "redial." I remembered all the letters the clerk had handed my mother when she had checked out of the boardinghouse so many years before.

During what seemed like unending days of waiting, I also went out for walks. One afternoon, I decided to walk around the complex of hospitals and office buildings at the center of town rather than through the nearby parks. Outside of the building where we had spent most of our time, there was an open area with paved sidewalks where kids skateboarded and mothers pushed strollers. And there in front of me was the original hospital building. It is topped by a distinctive terra cotta-trimmed tower that contains a fifty-six bell carillon. Several times a week, songs that can be heard throughout downtown are played from it. The large bronze doors stand sixteen feet high and are five-and-a-half inches thick, consisting of forty-two 18 × 21-inch panels. The Mayo Clinic's web site tells me that... "Six repeating symbolic panels and 2 repeating ornamental patterns are interspersed throughout each door. The symbolic panels show a woman kneeling next to her child to represent maternity and the home, a figure holding an overflowing cornucopia and a shock of wheat to represent agriculture, a figure with a paint palette and brushes to represent the fine arts, a figure with a lamp and scroll to represent education, and a figure with a hook and crane to represent the mechanical arts. The ornamental panels have a central button surrounded by floral patterns and smaller etchings of flora and fauna, such as squirrels, pinecones, indigenous to Minnesota." The deep, arched doorways were surrounded with carvings and curlicues.

Though it was Saturday, the doors were unlocked. I walked through the bronze doors into what must now have become administrative offices, and I tried to picture my mother in this same place fifty-five years before. The halls had marble floors and closed, thick wooden doors. Had these once been bustling hallways with crisp, white-uniformed nurses hurrying into rooms? At Christmastime, did townspeople sing carols to the patients?

Early on Sunday morning, on one of my walks, I passed a church that had a labyrinth in its courtyard. I carried my mother in my heart as I walked the labyrinth; I was struggling with, and rebelling against, the overwhelming task I was facing alone. As I neared the end, the words of the hymn "Have Thine own Way, Lord. Have Thine own way. You are the potter. I am the clay" gently wound their way through my soul. I was able to give myself over in surrender to what lay in store for me.

Our paths did not end in the same place. Becca's cancer never returned, while Mike's took his life. I do know my mother was walking this path with me. My sermonette in Mercedes's little church, about God's having his own way, was a reprise of a trying time both for my mother and for me in cold Minnesota.

Chapter 12
The School at Llano Grande

The next morning Mercedes and I push her grandson Hugito, son of her younger daughter Esthela, in the stroller down the rutted road leading to the former mission school near the church. In spite of the sunshine, a brisk breeze is blowing. Mercedes is caring for her grandson while his mother works today. At the end of the road, we find the gate to the school open and walk into the playground, where children in uniforms are kicking soccer balls to one another. The school is now a public school, but at the insistence of its former graduates, it is still named Escuela Brethren. The thick-walled adobe buildings I remember have been replaced by large, airy classrooms, but they still sit along the retaining walls that surround the playground. I ask one of the teachers to take a picture of Mercedes and me standing on the cistern, just as we stand in the yellowed photograph in my album, taken when we were just twelve years old.

Two years after establishing themselves in Ecuador, the missionaries opened an elementary school in Llano Grande. The remaining walls of an old hacienda house were repaired and whitewashed. Rafters of tall, slender eucalyptus trunks were nailed into place, and bundles of red tiles were passed up, bucket-brigade style, to workers who overlapped them on the rafters.

The missionaries visited families in the community, inviting them to enroll their children in the school, and that first year, six little boys were enrolled in first grade. A few weeks into the school year, the grandmother of one of the boys died. The Roman Catholic priest refused to bury her if the boy continued to attend the mission school, so five little boys finished out the year.

Although I did not attend the mission school, instead going to a school for missionaries' children in Quito, I do remember the community's excitement when the national department of education came to test the Brethren school students. At the end of each school year, inspectors came out from Quito to administer examinations. The children, dressed in their uniforms, and their parents, wearing their best clothes, gathered in the school courtyard. The little pump organ was moved out onto the veranda so that when the inspectors arrived, the children could line up and sing the Ecuadorian national anthem, "*Sale, o Patria, mil vezes, o Patria, Gloria a Tí, Gloria a Tí.*" Then they filed into the chapel. I joined the parents, teachers, missionaries, and community leaders who gathered on the chapel benches. The inspectors sat at a long table in front, while the children sat on small chairs on the platform.

At my school, I was working my way through the "Dick and Jane" readers, so I was amazed to hear my little peers answering the questions about civics and geography that the inspectors asked. To make sure this was not just rote memorization, one of the inspectors pulled out that morning's edition of *El Comercio*, the major Ecuadorian daily newspaper. I held my breath as he handed it to the first little boy; then, to my amazement, the child stepped forward, looked out at his parents, and began to read that day's news. The inspectors were equally amazed to see how well the indigenous children had learned.

When the testing was done, the children put on a program for the parents and the inspectors. There were songs, recitation of poems, and skits. I remember one poem that started, "*Porque era el niño con tanta gravidad...*" "Why was the child so serious..." The child's face took on a look of grief as he recited the long poem about a child whose mother was ill. Songs celebrated the beauty of the country of Ecuador.

A little girl and boy got up to perform a skit. The girl carried a doll around the stage, rocking it in her arms. The boy sang, "*¿Señora Santana, porque llora el niño?* Mrs. Santana, why is your baby crying?"

She sang back, "*Por una manzana que se le ha perdido.* For an apple that he lost."

The boy responded, "*Ven a mi casa. Yo te daré dos. Una para el niño y ortra para vos.* Come to my house. I will give you two, one for the baby and one for you." With that, the boy pretended to punch the girl and her doll in their faces. The audience roared with laughter at the double meaning of manzana: apple and "goose egg."

After the program, everyone gathered in the courtyard and in the school dining room for a meal of boiled potatoes and corn on the cob with hot peanut sauce. There was also *come y bebe*, eat and drink, my favorite beverage at such festivities. There were two whole barrels of punch containing a case of mineral water, thirty bananas, two large papayas, one hundred oranges and two hundred lemons, and we drank it from large tin cups, eating the pieces of fruit that floated in the juice and celebrating how well the school had done on the examination.

The second year of the school, the first five boys went on to second grade and seventeen more children started in first grade. Mercedes was one of those children.

Today Mercedes and I decide to take a stroll through the woods behind the school, where eucalyptus trees and cabuyas still dot the hillside. As birds sing, Hugito falls asleep to the bumping of the path. Returning to rest at the old cistern, we sit down on a nearby wall. Mercedes tells me what she recalls about that year.

"When we went to enroll, I wore my embroidered blouse, my *anako*—the wool wraparound skirt—the whole outfit. But when we got there, we were told not to wear that, that we needed to wear a skirt and blouse."

I ask Mercedes about why the children were not allowed to wear their native clothes, and she tells me that the teacher, an educated indigenous man, thought the children would have a better chance to get ahead if they dressed like whites. He even insisted that the boys have their *wangos*, single pigtails, cut off. "So your father got you the new clothes?" I ask.

"Yes. And you know what I did? My father said, 'You must get ready. It is only fifteen days until school starts.' I did not want to go for anything. In the community they said that the *gringos* made sausages out of children. So, I did not want to become a sausage." We both laugh. "I did not want to go, but my father said, 'No, they are good people, and they will treat you well.' I suppose it was because he had worked for missionaries at HCJB when he was twelve.

"I imagine that my father had accepted the Lord at that time because he was always very different. He did not drink; he always worked in the community, in the mingas. He would take us along to work with little tools that he made for us."

"Little tools for the little ones…" I say. I can picture her father with the three little children, each with his or her own tool.

"When he heard those comments people made, he would say, 'You don't know what the gringos are like. They are good. They will like you a lot.' On the other hand, my grandma said, 'Be careful if you go because they will make sausage out of you. They are devils, gringos.' She didn't even know what they were."

"But your father didn't listen to her." I don't remember this woman, Tia Maria's mother.

"No. My father bought shoes—he had bought men's shoes—and a skirt and blouse and something for my hair, to make braids because I had a wango. Well, I thought, 'Perhaps if he can't find the clothes, he won't send me to school.' So, I went into the woods where there were reeds growing and I made a hole and buried my clothes, everything that he bought for school. That Saturday, he said to my mother, 'Maria, prepare the clothes for Mercedes because Monday she needs to go to school.' I was nervous. My mother went into the room to look for the clothes. We had two rooms, one for sleeping and one for cooking. There was no way to lose something. She went to the trunk and opened it. But, no clothes! My mother looked everywhere. She looked and looked until there was nowhere else to look. Then, with great fear—she feared my father even though he was not mean, but with great respect, she told him, 'You know, I can't find the clothes.' 'Impossible,' he said. 'They must be here.' So, he looked too and didn't find them."

"He must have been so mad." I smiled at her as she recalled those childhood years. I knew that her father had many sides to him.

"What an expression I must have had! 'What did you do with the clothes?' he asked, and I couldn't say anything. He asked me at least four times, but I didn't say anything. So, he went out to the edge of the patio to look for a stick, and I knew I was going to be punished. He came in and said, 'What did you do with the clothes?' I began to yell and squeal. 'Ahiii!' I screamed. 'It's because you are going to take me to the gringos who make sausage out of children, and I don't want to go. So I hid my clothes out there.' My father went digging and found the clothes and they had to wash them that very day. I suppose it was sunny because they were dry by Monday."

"So now you were ready to go," I say. It is a sunny day like it must have been that September day when school started for her so many years ago. The wind brushes our faces. Hugito stirs but finds his pacifier and goes back to sleep.

"I was very frightened as I went to school. Usually I wore an anako that came down to here, very warm when it was cold, when it's sunny, it's okay, so I went in my skirt and men's shoes that I couldn't walk in, with my hair braided by my mother. But what a surprise! I remember your mother Señora Ruby meeting us with a smile. It relieved my fear a bit when she received us, explained where the patio was and where the classes were. Then the bell rang and there were twenty-two of us. It was the second year of the school. They explained where we were to line up, and I thought it was so strange to see everyone dressed like me because they had told everyone not to come in Llano Grande clothing."

I shake my head. I still don't really understand why they were told not to wear their beautiful native clothing.

"It was such a surprise for me, such a great impact, the love they showed us. When I got home, my father asked how it went. I said, 'It went well. They are good people.' 'You see?' he said. 'See what I said? They are good people. You should not be afraid.'

"That very day—I was already eight years old—I looked at the teacher and I said, 'I want to be like him. I want to be a teacher like him.' I decided then that I wanted to be a teacher, and I struggled so hard to achieve what I wanted."

I nod. "And you did eventually study at the university and became a teacher." She smiles and nods.

"The teacher taught us to sing. He was musical. He composed music and played the clarinet. That day, we spent almost the whole day singing, playing, and talking. I was enchanted with school and couldn't wait to go back. The morning couldn't come soon enough so that I could go to school."

Hugito begins to fuss, so we get up and walk with the stroller into one of the school buildings. Windows fill the large classrooms with light. Nobody notices us; they are all too busy with their work in the classrooms. Uniformed children bend over their desks. Teachers walk among the desks or stand in front of blackboards.

Mercedes continues. "Now, up to then, I attended the Catholic Church all the time. My father wasn't pleased with that and didn't want us to go. Even as a young child, I helped with construction of that Catholic church because I had such respect for the Christian religion. I would gather my younger brothers. They knew how to whistle to call the other children our age so we could all go to catechism every afternoon. We hurried home from school, and my father, who didn't want us to go, always had tasks for us: pulling weeds for the rabbits, feeding the pigs, feeding the chickens and little chicks, doing something in the soil, all to keep us from going to catechism. But the three of us, even my little brother helped, worked together so that we could go with the other children from the community."

"The Catholic Church…" I recall the hostility that we had experienced from the Catholic priest and the nuns. It had cast such a shadow on my parents' time in Ecuador. We stop to admire students' work on a bulletin board then make our way outside. The baby drifts off to sleep again as we reach the edge of the school grounds. It seems we have all of the time in the world out here.

"At the church, the priest taught us. He talked so much about hell and had a huge picture of fire and suffering. One day, I said, 'Why did God create us if he was going to condemn us that way? It isn't just.' But I continued to go anyway. However, since we attended the mission school, one day the priest said, 'We don't want the children who attend that devils' school to attend catechism here.' Since that day, I never went back to the Catholic Church. I no longer invited the neighborhood children to come. In time, your mother invited us to come to Sunday school. We listened for the church bell. I don't know if it was so loud or if there was not so much other noise. We heard it all the way at our house. Ever since, I have always loved the music of bells."

"And I remember ringing that bell. It was on top of a tall pole and had a rope that we pulled to make it ring." We walk toward the open gate near the school. A soccer ball whizzes by. A teacher coaching some boys in the yard nods at us as we leave. We start back up the road, past the houses and small shops.

Mercedes wants to speak more about those days when their family was moving into the missionaries' church. "'It is nine o'clock,' I would say to my father on a Sunday. 'Señora Ruby invited us to come on Sundays to hear teachings about Jesus. I want to go.' We never did anything without my parents' permission. With my father's permission, we started to attend. At first, it was only me and my brothers, but we shared everything that we learned with my father and mother. Eventually, my parents also came, and the three of us were all baptized. My brothers were still small."

"You were the first people from the community to be baptized," I say as we walk along the dusty path toward home. "Others followed, Pedro and Segundo, the miller from Calderon…"

"After I broke things off with the Catholic Church, we began to suffer persecution. They didn't even want to see us at the mingas. Nothing, nothing. We were totally outside because they said we were devils, too. 'Be careful about hanging around with those devils.' So, that left my family all alone. We attended church and that helped us a lot. We had Bible studies in our house and we invited neighbors.

"I invited this one man who had said we shouldn't go. I invited him and, wow, he got so mad. 'Impossible! How is it possible that you invite me to meet with those devils?' he said. 'I belong to the *virgencita*, little Virgin Mary, the Virgin of Quinche. Don't be so naughty.' I never again invited him and he was a *compadre*, godfather, of my father."

My father recalled in his memoirs his first encounter with the local priest. Soon after arriving in Llano Grande, he was summoned by the local priest. He went immediately, hoping to get acquainted. His account of the encounter according to his memoir follows:

An uncomfortable conversation...

"What is your purpose in coming here? What do you plan to do?"

"Our purpose is to serve the Indian people of Llano Grande. We understand that almost all are illiterate and that there is no school. We propose to open a school."

The priest bristled. "The people may be ignorant. But whatever they need to know, I will tell them. That is my job."

I continued, "We understand that there is no medical service here—no doctor, no nurse for some ten thousand people. Is that so?"

He answered, "The reason for their illnesses is mostly connected to their drinking and eating habits. If they are sick, it is their own fault."

"We would like to bring a doctor and nurse to this valley," I said. "We also hope to help them farm better on their small plots and to improve their livestock."

Then came the real sixty-four dollar question for which I had been summoned. "Do you expect to start a church?"

My answer, "We expect to teach the Bible to any and all who wish to know about the scriptures. If that should lead the people to form a church, then I would consider it the work of the Holy Spirit."

The priest squirmed in his chair. He was furious and shot back with "These souls are mine. When thieves came into the temple, Jesus drove them out with a whip and I am not greater than my Lord." I was taken aback. I had thought, naively I guess, that this was to be a friendly get-acquainted—even perhaps the beginning of some joint effort on behalf of the people. It was not to be.

As we head back towards Elizabeth's house, I tell Mercedes my own initial experience with persecution was hearing the nuns tell their schoolchildren to throw sticks and stones at us as they met us along the road. Once the mission school was established, the Catholics also started one to compete. I suppose, though, that the children of the community benefitted because now there were two schools where there had been none.

I did fear for my father, though. One evening, when he was

attending a Bible study at Mercedes's home, there was a knock on the door. Her father Pedro went to the door and saw that there were some men from the neighborhood, so he invited them to come in and join the Bible study. They held torches and rocks in their hands, and Mercedes feared that they would burn down the house. She says, "My father had made shocks of corn and had them all around the house under the eaves so they would not get wet. They were going to light them with all of us in the house. There were ugly rumors that my mother was naked inside with the devils that had come to preach."

Her father went out and saw among them some compadres of his. "Come in and study the word of God with us. Then, if you want to do something to us, do it. We are not afraid." Mercedes remembers that she was trembling with fear.

"'Send out the devils,' they said." My father and the other men in the house got up and went out into the patio. Dad recognized one of the men and greeted him by name, with an outstretched hand. Since men always shook hands when they met, the man automatically moved his rock into his left hand and shook my dad's hand. All of the men who had come out of the house followed suit. Around the circle of would-be attackers they went, shaking hands, and each man they reached out to had to transfer his rock or torch to the other hand to extend the expected polite greeting. That was that.

Just north of Calderon, the white community that housed the main Catholic Church, was another small indigenous community, San Miguel del Común. A few people from there had started venturing to the mission to learn weaving on the looms in the workshop and to attend church. Just as they were becoming skillful at weaving, they stopped coming. So, one evening, Dad took Segundo, a young indigenous friend of ours who could help translate the Kichwa language, and drove up to check on them. Dad didn't know that the family he went to visit had had a death in the family. The priest had threatened not to bury their family member if they continued to come to the textile workshop and to church. He had also started a rumor that Dad was going to take the body when he came, and as with every funeral, there had been heavy drinking in the community.

While Dad met with the family in their home, the church bell began to ring. Unbeknownst to Dad, the priest had instructed the people that, when the bell rang, they were to kill the devils. The noise outside the house changed from drunken revelry to angry shouts, and Dad and Segundo started to leave in the truck. The people, though, had dug a trench across the road leading out of the community. While Dad and Segundo tried to lay branches and stones across the trench, people beat on the truck with clubs. When they finally made it up to the highway, without the headlights that had been smashed with clubs, they ran into the cliff on the other side. Dad climbed up on the cab of the truck and tried to talk to the mob, but they responded with rocks and clods of dirt. A passing car picked Dad and Segundo up and took them into Quito to the police. While they were gone, the people broke all the glass in the truck and turned it over, planning to burn it.

At that time, my mother's parents and my teenaged aunt and uncle were visiting. When the men failed to come home, my mother, my grandfather, and another missionary went into Calderon. My grandfather described what happened in a *Gospel Messenger* article:

"When we arrived and learned what had happened, Ruby came back home for a couple of the teachers and some flashlights. With a population of 500 or 600, the village of Calderon has no streetlights or electricity. Kerosene lanterns with an occasional gas lantern furnish their only light. There was something almost terrifying to be there in total darkness not knowing who were friendly and who were hostile. Ruby mingled with the crowd and talked to them. All expressed friendship for her, although a couple of women let it be known rather loudly that their sympathies were entirely with the Catholics."

Shortly after this incident, the reality of persecution came home for me. The next evening, Mario, the hired man, came back from Calderon and said that a mob was forming to come and attack the mission. He said that the mob was excited and angry and that liquor was flowing freely. The teachers from the school, the children of a Calderon family who were church members, and a number of people from Llano Grande gathered on the porch of the mission house that was closest to the woods.

It was dark and the electric generator was turned off. We pulled blankets around our shoulders against the cold night air. Shivering, we whispered about how we would escape through the woods and down the path to the quebrada, then up the hill to the small town on the other side and out the road to safety. I remembered hiking down that path and up to the village on the other side in daylight but could not imagine doing it at night. Jan complained of leg pain, "growing pains," and the adults discussed having someone carry her. My aunt entertained us with her renditions of current popular music while my uncle did algebra problems.

That whole time we kept watch, looking toward the road and listening for any signs of an approaching mob, while several men went up the road to watch. A blast from their shotgun would be our signal to escape through the woods. We waited until well after midnight, when we got word that there were police in Calderon and the mob had dispersed. Reluctantly, we returned to our house and tried to go to sleep. No one slept well that night.

Over the years, the members of the church continued to experience discrimination. Mercedes tells me that when her brother Enrique fell in love with Laura, a Catholic girl, the girl's parents hid her from him to keep her from marrying an *evangelico*, or Protestant. With the election of Pope John XXIII, more cordial relations were possible. He met personally with evangelicals and prayed with them, asking them to pray for him and referring to them as "separated Brethren."

That road where we had watched fearfully for attacks from angry and inebriated townspeople is the very road we now walk along, pushing the baby, returning to Elizabeth's home.

Chapter 13
Aunt Edith: The Missionary School

I was encouraged that the present-day school continues to be called Escuela Brethren at the request of its many graduates whose lives were touched by their time as students there. My own schooling was in a different school. We missionary children attended the School for Missionary Children in Quito, which utilized North American curriculum so that we could more easily transition back to U.S. schools whenever we were on furlough.

In 1947 Dad wrote to the Mission Board, "Near the end of the present five-year period, we will need to arrange for starting formal education of missionary children. There is the possibility of making application to the Christian and Missionary Alliance boarding school in Quito, which is a school of very high scholastic standing. If our children are accepted there, we would still have to consider the matter of fundamentalist pressure upon them. This might be counteracted by our Board volunteering to furnish a teacher on their staff or by our having a home or house-mother in Quito and sending our children as day students. The school is located on the edge of Quito nearest Calderón which means that it is only about 14 miles from Bella Vista [the mission farm], which might even be considered as a daily commuting distance. The other alternative to applying to the C.M.A. school would be for our mission to send a worker whose main task would be the formal education of our children. A third alternative, of course, would be for each family to educate its own children in the home, which is probably not too satisfactory."

Most missionaries work to help the native people and bring them the good news of the gospel. Then there are those whose work it is to bring the good news to the children of those missionaries. They worked as teachers in the School for Missionary Children and as houseparents in boarding homes for kids who lived too far away to travel to school daily, and a part of that calling in my school was instruction, and lots of it, in their faith.

They left nothing to chance. At school, every day started with Bible class, and there was a place for our Bible grade on our report cards. A lot of the grade depended on one's ability to memorize scriptures; I have never been good at memorizing, so while I might otherwise have made the honor roll, there were times when my Bible grade kept me off of it. In my first and second grade room, we each had a long ribbon hanging along the wall. As we committed a passage to memory, we got a paper cutout picture to represent it on the ribbon. There was a shield for "putting on the armor of God," a trumpet for the angel's announcement to the shepherds, and, of course, a sheep for the Twenty-Third Psalm. The sheep was the only picture that ever made it onto my ribbon because Aunt Betty had made us a cross-stitch wall hanging with the Twenty-Third Psalm that hung in our dining room, where I looked at it during meals and gradually learned the scripture.

Each Monday morning, instead of Bible class, the whole school attended chapel together, complete with flannel-graphs, light blue flannel, mounted on a board supported by an easel. Onto the flannel were pressed pictures, backed with sandpaper so they would stick. There were pictures of the wide path to hell, peopled with gaily dressed folks dancing, smoking, and drinking, and of the straight and narrow path to heaven, where primly dressed people knelt to pray or read their Bible. Then there were people being snatched up into glory or being left behind on the Day of Judgment, and we all knew where they went.

This would be followed by a call to raise your hand, first if you were already saved, then if you wanted to be saved. Well, I figured that I was a pretty good girl, so I raised my hand that I was saved. But, then came the question, "Do you want to be saved?" Well, sure. If I'm not saved, then I do want to be saved. So, up went my hand.

Now the clincher. "If you want to be saved, please meet in the principal's office after chapel." A brief wait outside the principal's door (it felt like an eternity) convinced me there had to be a better way.

The following weekend, when I was home, I talked it over with Dad, a missionary who spread the gospel by his actions, providing education, medical care, and development training, and using words only when needed. He sighed and said, "I think I would ask them, 'Saved from what and for what?'" That answer provided me with a ready reply, though I am not sure if I ever used it.

Many of the children at the school came from great distances and boarded at the school. Kids whose parents worked in Peru or Colombia only made it home for summer vacation. We were luckier and were able to live at home most of the time. Someone at the mission drove all of the missionary children to and from school every day, which required one missionary to spend at least two hours a day since the drive took a half hour each way. If they were bringing several of us, it was worth making the trip. When I was in fifth grade, however, my sister Jan and I were the only children coming to school from the mission, because that year the other family with school-age children was on furlough in the States. So we went to stay at the GMU (Gospel Missionary Union) house, a few blocks from school. The housemother there was Aunt Edith, a matronly single woman who ran a tight ship.

Jan roomed in a big room full of bunk beds with seven or eight other girls. Since I was the second oldest girl in the house, I got placed in a room with Janice, a high school girl. Janice wore starched can-can half-slips and wide, tight belts that gave her figure the coveted wasp waist. Her teenaged brother Jack had the room downstairs from ours. He had a record player and had run a wire up to our room through the window to attach to a speaker, so in the evenings, we could listen to Nat King Cole singing "Mona Lisa" and "Arrivederci Roma" and other popular favorites. Listening to this kind of music was considered to be sinful because it might lead to dancing and, everyone knew, dancing led to sex and other sins. I'm not sure how they slipped that one by Aunt Edith; perhaps she was just too busy keeping track of all the younger children to pay attention.

Aunt Edith's way of managing our medical needs was unique,

to say the least. There was the milk of magnesia, used to treat most anything and also used to get stool samples for our annual parasite tests. Unfortunately, the milk of magnesia didn't get the desired results from me, and my stools never got soft enough to be sent for examination. So, every night after prayers, I was sent to the kitchen, where I tried, unsuccessfully, to gag down a glass of Epsom salts mixed with *naranjilla* juice. I would hold my nose and bring it to my lips, only to rush to the sink and pour it down the drain. It took several weeks for me to finally drink the awful mixture, and I still think I smell Epsom salts mixed with naranjilla when I drink from an anodized aluminum tumbler.

When I got pinkeye from the shared towel in the school restroom, Aunt Edith came into my room and said, "You are always the first one to get everything." I actually think it was the first time I had gotten sick. This could not be treated with milk of magnesia; it required quarantine. I was only allowed out of my room to go to the bathroom, where I, of course, shared the same hand/face towel with the other girls in the house. While they were at school, I was allowed go downstairs and listen to records or look at books. On the day that Aunt Edith went to market, my sister and her friends all came down with "tummy aches" and had to stay home from school. After dosing them all with milk of magnesia, Aunt Edith left for the market, and they came into my room to visit. It wasn't long until everyone else in the house had pinkeye.

Then kids at school started getting mumps. One night, I woke up with sore ears and neck and I could feel lumps under my jaws. I got up, went into the bathroom and turned on the light, and there in the mirror, I confirmed my worst fears: I had mumps. I crept back into bed and laid there with tears streaming down my cheeks. I knew what Aunt Edith would say when she saw me in the morning. When she was told, she sent word for me to stay in my room until the other kids left for school, then she came into my room, her hands sternly on her hips. "You are always the first one to get everything." This time, it was true, and this time, she had learned her lesson. I was confined to my room at all times. A little chamber pot was even brought into the room. Meals were brought up to me, and only my roommate Janice was allowed into the room. She, miraculously, did not get mumps. Although she rarely talked with me, a lowly fifth-grader, she did take her Tiny Tears doll out of her trunk and let me play with it when I felt like it. But, mostly I felt really sick, feverish and sore. I tossed in bed with fever-induced nightmares, and it felt like forever.

My parents did not have a phone for someone to let them know that I was sick, and Aunt Edith didn't send anyone to tell them. One day, though, after "forever," my mother showed up at the door of the house. She had been in town shopping and met someone who told her I was sick.

"Is Jeannie sick?" she demanded. "Why didn't anyone let us know?"

"We're taking good care of her. You didn't need to be called," said Aunt Edith.

"I would have wanted her with me if she is sick."

Mom immediately took me home, and I spent the rest of my mumps time resting in the sunny porch and enjoying the warmth of my mother's presence. My brother Bobby did get mumps, but none of the kids at the boardinghouse came down with the disease after I left.

Aunt Edith's rules were stricter than I was used to at home. We were not allowed to wear short-sleeved blouses or pedal pushers because we might tempt sin by showing our elbows or our knees. When we played outside and she was busy in the house, we rolled up our sleeves and pant legs. How delicious to be able to break the rules in such an innocent way!

If one of the children misbehaved, Aunt Edith would send the child out to find a green branch and bring it to her. That child hunting for the switch was often my roommate Janice's younger brother Jimmy, who just couldn't seem to obey the rules. If the branch he brought met her inspection, strong but flexible, Jimmy was flogged in front of all the other children. We all must learn the lesson, along with poor Jimmy. No one tried to stop her, and I don't know if Janice ever told her parents. Perhaps they would have approved.

In our free time, Aunt Edith encouraged us to play church. We would sit in the library and sing, "This world's not my home, I'm just a' passing through," and "preach" from the magazines that were on the shelves. I don't know if she realized it, but we also were getting our first exposure to nude photos in the *National Geographic* magazines that filled those same shelves. Most of us knew exactly where in the magazine to find the pictures of naked men and women with just a string around their waists, standing in a jungle somewhere in the world. Of course, Aunt Edith hoped that each of us would also become a missionary, and so we read books about missionaries and talked about where we planned to go. I planned to go to Tibet and learned all I could about the country, which seemed so strange and exotic. Never did it cross my mind that others might think I was already living a strange and exotic life in Ecuador.

Aunt Edith tried to temper her strictness with her own kind of mothering. On Jan's and my first evening at the house, she invited us to come sit on her lap to help us "feel more at home." Her lap was cushiony, but I felt awkward, too big and too old, to be sitting on this strange woman's lap. It absolutely did *not* make me feel at home.

She also would invite each little girl, individually, to sleep overnight with her. I suppose she was trying to temper her strictness with a little bit of warmth. When my turn was coming up, I asked the other girls what I should expect. "She uses a hot water bottle to keep her feet warm, and she lets you use it until she gets into bed. She turns off the light in the room to get into her nightgown so that no one can look in the window and see her changing clothes, but I think it is really so that we can't see her." So I went to Aunt Edith's overnight. I stiffened as she climbed into bed, but she slept clear on the other side of the bed. Awake most of the night, I anxiously awaited the first rays of sun through the window. By the time I woke up, she had already gotten up and dressed. My turn was over, and I hoped that it would never come around again.

Breakfast was usually oatmeal, homemade Grape-Nuts, or *machica*, a powder of toasted and ground barley that we ate with milk. On Sundays, though, we had eggs, which were more expensive and saved for the special day. One of the children was assigned each morning to get up early and help set the two long tables that stretched down the sides of the dining room. Each child sat at his or her assigned place, all in church clothes with clean faces and neatly combed hair.

One Sunday, just as we were ready to start eating, a little Ecuadorian girl came to the kitchen door wanting to sell a chicken. Seeing an opportunity to teach all the little missionary kids a lesson, Aunt Edith had the cook send the girl into the dining room. She was barefoot and her tattered dress hung loosely on her thin frame, and there she stood in front of us with her eyes cast down to the floor. Timidly she faced all these clean, healthy white kids eating their eggs for breakfast. Aunt Edith scolded her. "It is Sunday. It is a sin to sell things on Sunday. The Bible says 'remember the Sabbath to keep it holy.' The wages of sin is death. Take your chicken and go home, and don't try to sell on Sunday again." We sat aghast, wondering if the little girl might be trying to make money for medication for a sick mother, or if she even had a mother.

Aunt Edith was teaching us a lesson, but not the one she thought she was teaching. These zealous missionaries to the missionary kids taught me to have a healthy skepticism for all things "religious." I have to say that I am still a Christian, in spite of, not because of, their teaching.

Chapter 14
Nurturing and Being Nurtured by the Church

It was in the little mission church in Llano Grande that my faith was nurtured. That faith was confirmed for life in spite of what happened at the zealot boarding school.

My earliest memories of church are the mid-week prayer meetings in the little chapel behind the school. An old hacienda building was slowly being restored to house the mission school. The hacienda had fallen into great disrepair and needed a new roof and plaster and paint. In the back, there was a small chapel, probably used by the previous owners for Catholic mass. The statue of Mary was gone from its niche in the wall, and we replaced it with a picture of Jesus. The adobe walls smelled of freshly applied whitewash. The ceiling was esteras, reed mats like those used in local homes for sleeping. And this little building became our first, tiny, church.

Jan and I sat on backless wooden benches in the front row: two scrubbed and starched little blond girls among the native girls with their brightly embroidered blouses, black wool skirts, and shawls over their straight black braids. We sang at the top of our lungs from the pocket-size *Himnos de la Vida Christiano*, the little hymn book that had only the words of the hymns. When we had song selection, I always asked for "*O, santisimo, felicisimo*" ("Oh, how joyfully"), whether it was Christmas or not. And we always sang it.

Following our morning visit and long talk at the school, Mercedes and I have had an afternoon rest and a good meal at Elizabeth's house. As the sun sinks low, my old friend and I have returned to the current church building in the eucalyptus grove for the Monday evening Bible study and prayer meeting. A small group is gathered on the benches at the front of the church, and we join them. They are discussing how God responds to our prayers, followed by prayer requests. The youngest person there is a young man who asks for prayers for himself as he takes the medical school entrance exam. Mercedes asks for prayers for a friend. As we had walked to this church, she had recalled aloud how, long ago, she and her brothers would come hurrying to church when they heard music from the loudspeaker.

The little chapel had served only for a while. With the help of the community, one of the larger rooms of the hacienda that housed the new school was made into a sanctuary that doubled as the school auditorium. On Sunday mornings, we would dress in our cotton dresses and walk to church. Mom often commented on how proud she felt, walking behind her four little children along the path through the eucalyptus woods to church. When we arrived at the church, we opened the doors and shutters and put the manually cranked record player on the deep adobe window ledge. It was housed in a leather carrying case, and the crank fit into a slot under the turntable. After cranking it tight, I put a black vinyl record onto the turntable and carefully set the needle in its round arm down on the record. It wasn't quite a loudspeaker, but we did turn the volume up as high as we could. When the music began to slow, I again turned the crank.

Sitting on the wooden pews of the current church building, Mercedes and I wait just a moment after everybody leaves. That old school auditorium worship place has been replaced by a real, small church of its own. I recall my pleasure in yesterday's modern-feeling church service in this place. Time has moved on; seeds that we sowed as missionaries have sprouted and grown. The light is fading in the old eucalyptus grove, and a chill breeze drifts through the many glass windows. Outside, the wind makes the clapper of the original church bell softly bump the bell on the pole. Inside, we hug our ponchos and shawls around us and squeeze together for warmth.

I recall that Mercedes's family was the first to join the church, boldly choosing it just as they had chosen to go to school. Her father had become acquainted with Protestants when he worked as a houseboy for missionaries in Quito, causing him to be more open than others in the community to coming to church. Over time, Mercedes's family became leaders in the church, as they still are to this day. Her father Pedro worked with my father and learned all he could to help pastor the church.

> **In an article in the *Gospel Messenger*, this devoted Christian Pedro described his life to my father:**
>
> It seems now that God willed it that, when a boy of eleven, I should go to work in the house of Señor David (one of the early Protestant missionaries in Quito). As house boy it fell my lot to make the long hard journey to the coastal plain with them for vacation once. Having never left our little mountain community, I was afraid. Surely such a journey would take us to the very end of the world. Where would we eat? Where could we sleep? I asked Señor David, who told me I should have no fears. At night fall, we arrived at the house of people who seemed to be expecting us and glad to see us. We went in like relatives and the same thing happened night after night along the way. From then I knew that believers are brothers and even more than brothers.
>
> A few months later I left my job in the missionaries' home to search for work that would pay more. For my "papa" had been named preoste to pay for the mass and to foot the bill for a year of drinking on Catholic feast days in our community. We boys must work and give all to help him. But even so, the costs were too heavy. Father went in debt. We lived in a borrowed house the rest of his life. From that time on we, his sons, followed in his footsteps of drink and barely existing from one feast day to another. We wept, we drank, we fought and everyone thought we were real men.
>
> Then at eighteen, I was married. My father, a hopeless drunkard, gave me no counsel as Indian fathers should. But mother did. I got up at dawn one morning to help her twist ropes and to tell her of my desire to be married to Maria. "I know the girl," she said. "Buy enough ponchos and save money to buy her some skirts and some for

the babies that will come." The babies. I thought about that and when we were married I told Maria about how I had once known some people, Evangelicos, who raise their children in the fear of God and live spending their money for bread instead of chicha (beer). If we have a baby, be it boy or girl, we are going to get it educated by people like that. Maria declared that she had never known people like that. What religion could it be? But, being the wife, she passively consented in theory that day.

A married man must drink, drink lots, to be somebody in the Indian community. I fell to drink with a vengeance to prove myself a man and because I could not let it alone. The first baby came, then more. I went home from fiestas drunk, yelling, angry. I chased Maria from the house. She hid in the hedge with the children. O God, thank you that I was too drunk to find them! For one night I hunted them with a sharpened machete to kill them all—my family. I slept in fence rows. I did not know night from day. Yet everyone thought I was sane. Now some say I am crazy, when I pass on the road with my family, singing hymns or reading the Book.

Mercedes, our first, was of school age when we heard that foreigners had moved into the community, bought Bella Vista, and planned to start a school. Then we heard that the foreigners were Evangelicos and I remembered I had told Maria that people like that must educate our children. So I enrolled Mercedes in the school, but with no thought of going near there myself. But Maria went. I do not know what all happened, but Maria came home greatly moved. She wept and yet she was happy. She tried to tell me. I know now that Maria accepted the Lord in her heart that day. From then on we sent the children to Sunday school. They came home telling us the Bible stories, Sundays and week days alike. Mercedes preached to me, but I did not want to hear, especially when I was drinking or in a temper. At such times she, an eight-year-old, talked to me about the Christian life. She said she knew that life was for her. I agreed it was for her but not for me and consented that she follow it.

That is why Maria came to the school to say that Mercedes wanted to be an Evangelical Christian (the first in Llano Grande) and that we would not oppose her. We came to church that next Sunday to show our approval of Mercedes' choice. Although you, brother, had said it, we did not realize, until we walked forward with her that day and knelt to pray, that the Word was for all of us—that we could not present Mercedes, sending her on the Christian way alone.

> He was sharing a confidence with me as if I were an adult.
>
> I never thought then of being a pastor like you, brother, but I knew I was happiest when talking with Indians in our own Kichwa language about the gospel. Sometimes there would be only one or two interested. Other times larger groups gathered. Then I stood up and spoke.
>
> The night that we discussed my witnessing to my people in our native tongue here in the church and voted, I felt that I had suddenly passed up through all the tribal ranks to which our men aspire and was being called to a position far beyond them—to a rank which only God can confer. That is why I prayed that night that "this be God's voice calling me and not just us here talking."
>
> Now it is almost a year, brother, that we are in class like this. To study is hard for me, especially to know where in the Bible it finishes talking about one thing and starts talking of another. Preaching is still hard but now that I take my turn every other week it is becoming easier to know what to preach about and not wander. But I cannot be a great preacher. They will have to come up through the school, like my boys. What is easy for me, like lifting a thin shaving of wood, are the gospel conversations which we have among neighbors in my house when they come to buy groceries or in theirs when they call me to plow or play the harp or see a sick one. I always go when called, for at such times I feel I have more right to speak.

Home from church now, Mercedes and I sit in her daughter Elizabeth's living room, nibbling on parched corn and sipping narajilla juice and recalling the early days of the church. She says, "The hymn that I will always remember is the one that they sang as I was in the baptismal waters. It is *Hay un preciosos manantial* 'There is a fountain.' I will always remember that."

The words form in my mind also, in Spanish and in English. It has special meaning for Mercedes and I understand that.

Hay un precioso manantial,	There is a fountain filled with blood
la sangre de Emanuel,	drawn from Emmanuel's veins;
que purifica a cada cual	and sinners plunged beneath that flood
que se sumerge en él.	lose all their guilty stains.

"I was ten years old when I was baptized," Mercedes continues. "Now I wonder how many more eventually followed in being baptized. When were you baptized?" I remember when I came forward during an altar call. I was nine years old. I had watched my friend Mercedes being baptized, and I talked it over with my parents. Dad said he was eight when he was baptized, so it seemed that I was old enough to make that decision for myself. A few weeks later, during the Sunday service, Dad invited anyone who wanted to turn his or her life over to Jesus to come forward.

Even sitting in the front row, it seemed a long way to go forward. I shivered with apprehension and from the coolness of the thick mud walls and brick floor. The pump organ played and the congregation sang.

He decidido seguir a Cristo,	I have decided to follow Jesus;
he decidido seguir a Cristo	I have decided to follow Jesus;
He decidido seguir a Cristo,	I have decided to follow Jesus;
no vuelvo atrás, no vuelvo atrás	No turning back, no turning back.

Taking a deep breath, I got up from my seat and walked to the front of the church. There, along with others who also chose to come forward, I knelt while Dad and Pedro placed their hands on my head and prayed. The others attended membership classes in the evenings to prepare for baptism, but Dad and Mom instructed me at home.

A baptismal pool had been built behind the church. On the morning before a baptism, two barrels of water were placed over a fire to heat the frigid water. Mom had helped me choose a simple cotton dress to wear, and when it was my turn, I stepped down into the lukewarm water and into my dad's hand. Gently he guided me into the center of the little pool and, placing a hand on my head and another over my face, he dunked me three times into the water. *"En el nombre del Padre, el Hijo y el Espiritu Santo.* In the name of the Father, the Son and the Holy Ghost." In spite of my practice in the bathtub the night before, the helplessness and fear of being submersed filled me with wonder at the decision I had made. As I emerged from the water, the little pump organ that had been carried out to the baptismal pool began to play, and the congregation gathered by the pool began to sing.

Día feliz, cuando escogí	Oh, happy day, when I chose,
Servirte, mi Señor y Dios;	To serve you, my Lord and God.
Preciso es que mi gozo en Ti	Precisely because of my joy in you,
Lo muestres hoy con obra y voz	I show it now in words and deeds.
¡Soy feliz! ¡Soy feliz!	I am happy, I am happy
Y en tu favor me gozaré.	And in your favor I rejoice.

In the evening of this modern day in Llano Grande, a dog barks out on the street. A cool wind blows through the open window as I reach for another handful of parched corn. Elizabeth's son Ernesto has gone to bed, so our voices are hushed as we remember together.

"Do you remember that it was you who prayed for me as I came up from the water?" I ask.

"I don't remember," answers Mercedes.

"It was the custom that someone who was already baptized would pray for the new member," I say. "I will always remember that it was you who prayed for me as I came up from the water. And, do you remember that, after we were baptized, when we celebrated the Lord's Supper, your mother said to my mother, 'This is our daughters' first communion.' First communion was something so important in her Catholic background, so it was special that we were taking our first communion together."

"Oh, yes," she says. "Because back then we did not take communion until we were baptized."

Now, with my friend at my side again, I am taken back to that first communion. The communion we celebrated that evening was the traditional Church of the Brethren Love Feast. Though I am now Mennonite, I am still drawn back to the local Church of the Brethren on Maundy Thursday to celebrate the Love Feast in the fashion I remember from that first time in Llano Grande.

On that evening, the church benches had been pushed to the sides of the sanctuary. In the center of the room were two long tables with white tablecloths. Candles lit the tables, and we spoke in hushed voices. Mercedes and I found places beside each other on a bench at the women's table. After a light meal of "sop," bread soaked in beef broth, we listened to the reading from Luke 22. "*Este es mi cuerpo, que ahora es entregado por tí.* This is my body broken for you." We smiled at each other as we broke the unleavened bread and bit into it. "*Este vino es mi sangre, derramado por tí.* This is my blood, poured out for you." We sipped the grape juice from the little communion cups.

It is a tradition in the Church of the Brethren to conclude the Love Feast with foot washing. John 13 says, "Jesus got up from the table, took off his outer robe and tied a towel around himself. Then he poured water into a basin and began to wash the disciples' feet and to wipe them with the towel that was tied around him… He said, 'you also ought to wash one another's feet. For I have set you an example, that you also should do as I have done to you.'"

Basins of water and towels sat on the floor at the ends of the tables. As I slipped off my shoes and socks, I looked at the other feet around the table. Most were bare. So, following Jesus's example, I knelt and washed the feet of my friend, Mercedes.

Mercedes and I gather up the juice glasses and remaining parched corn and head to the kitchen. It is getting late, and we have a busy day ahead tomorrow. We will be walking through the community, visiting people and places that I may or may not remember. We embrace and say good night. Our feet will need the rest. These feet have walked a long way together, and there is still more walking to do.

Certificado de Bautismo
Jesús dijo:

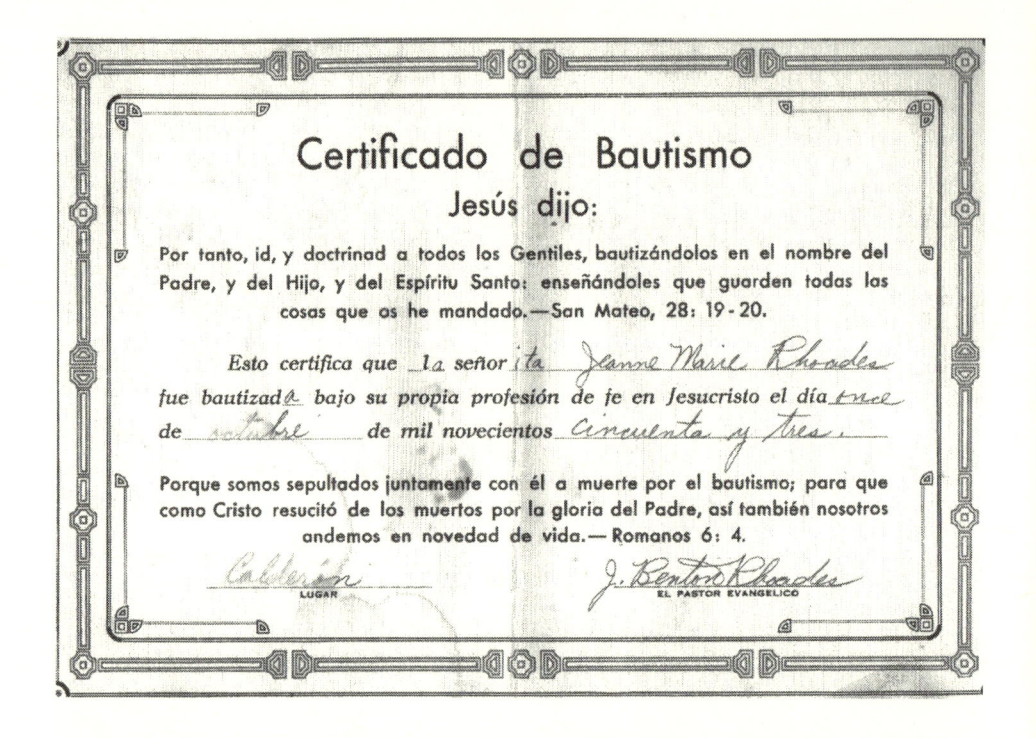

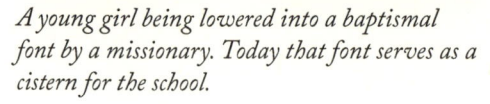

Por tanto, id, y doctrinad a todos los Gentiles, bautizándolos en el nombre del Padre, y del Hijo, y del Espíritu Santo; enseñándoles que guarden todas las cosas que os he mandado. — San Mateo, 28: 19-20.

Esto certifica que la señor*ita* *Jeanne Marie Rhoades* fue bautizad*a* bajo su propia profesión de fe en Jesucristo el día *once* de *octubre* de mil novecientos *cincuenta y tres*.

Porque somos sepultados juntamente con él a muerte por el bautismo; para que como Cristo resucitó de los muertos por la gloria del Padre, así también nosotros andemos en novedad de vida. — Romanos 6: 4.

Calderón
LUGAR

J. Benton Rhoades
EL PASTOR EVANGELICO

A young girl being lowered into a baptismal font by a missionary. Today that font serves as a cistern for the school.

Inside the Chapel worshippers solemnly listen to preaching. Many of them are new converts.

Students entered school in lines after singing the national anthem.

Boys and girls gave an excellent program after the National Examination.

MERCEDES TASIGUANO was a first-grade student last year in the mission school at Calderon near Quito, Ecuador. She and many other Indian children are looking to our mission personnel not only for classroom instruction but also to hear the good news about Jesus Christ and his gospel that affects all of life. *from* Gospel Messenger

Bulls plowed the fields. The ministry hoped to introduce modern farming methods.

Chapter 15
Sex Education

In the background of my experiences in Ecuador, both when I was a child and now as I return, is the relationship of men and women throughout South America. Beneath the superficialities of happily married lives is a layer of unhappiness, *machismo*, infidelity, and even abuse, perhaps not universal, but certainly prevalent. They are not alone in this situation, and of course, the relations of the sexes are, as everywhere else, in the eye of the storm.

A bright new day has dawned on my trip back to the neighborhood of my youth. I am sitting at the table in Mercedes's house. I'm thinking of that church we visited last night and the troubles it came to face, and I remember another bright morning in our family's mission home here, a day that turned out quite darkly. Because of incidents in the village, my mother felt she had to tell Jan and me about sexual intercourse on that morning long ago. Though the way it happened was abrupt and jarring, it was expected that a day would come when my sister Jan and I would be growing up and need to have instructions for adulthood. As difficult as this discussion always is for a mother to have with her daughters, my mother was from the first generation to have access to published information on the subject. Just a few years before her marriage to my father, before Masters and Johnson's groundbreaking research "liberated sex from the closet," a few publications had begun to address the subject openly. One such book purported to provide the "naked truth… stripped of all prudery and narrow prejudice. Old fashioned taboos are discarded and the subject of sex is brought out into the bright light of medical science."

I would imagine that my mother was referring to such a book when, just before her marriage, she wrote to her parents, "My fears are gradually being lessened and besides when I think of the millions of years that people had no medical advice, I'm pretty convinced that Benton and I shall make out satisfactorily. We've both read at least two books and we've read one together. We've been very frank in discussing such matters and I'm sure that will make it easier for both of us."

In another letter to her parents with plans for her wedding, Mom described an encounter with a less enlightened doctor in the hills straddling the border of Kentucky and West Virginia, where she and Dad were working the year they got married. "Yesterday I went to a doctor to talk about contraception, etc. It was such an unsatisfactory visit that I'm rather disgusted with the whole subject. From reliable sources I picked out the 'best' doctor in Williamson. Apparently, the poor fellow wasn't used to pre-marital counseling and I think he was almost embarrassed. All the books we had read, recommended having the hymen clipped and so I had planned to have that done, but I felt sorry for the poor embarrassed fellow and distrustful of his ability so I said nothing. He suggested as the *best* contraception is rubbers, I guess for men. When I asked about a diaphragm, he dismissed the subject by saying that they couldn't be inserted in a virgin. Heavens, what do I do now? We'll have to do something…Gosh, I need someone to talk to. Benton and I talked it all over, but there's nothing more he knows than I."

In spite of having this level of openness, my mother had to refer to resources that were filled with euphemisms and veiled statements that only hinted at facts. These "facts" were supposed to spare young people from having to "pay the awful price for one moment of bliss." In the old publications I found on the internet, sex was described with a range from "love is the most magnificent ecstasy in the world" to sex and sexual satisfaction being "the most powerful forces in your life." The morning Mom told us about human sex, I also remember her using the image of fire, a source of light and warmth but also a powerful destructive force if not properly harnessed. I know that she had imagined telling her daughters "the facts of life" in the context of light and warmth, not like this—a powerful destructive force, which is how it actually occurred at our mission in Ecuador that day.

Because we lived on the rural mission farm, we did have ample early introduction to the mechanics of biological reproduction, though it would take more deliberate efforts to help us make the connections between what we saw in the animal world and human sexuality. Everyone in the community had at least one dog, and there were also many strays. Our dog Lucha spent the day tethered to her doghouse under the cypress tree by the garden gate. At night, she was let loose to roam the farm and scare off possible intruders. The first time I saw a stray dog come into our yard and mount her, I was afraid that they were fighting. The many stray dogs in the community often fought over the limited food they were able to find. I still find it jarring to see and hear dogs fighting. Seeing dogs mating on that farm, though, became routine to us.

At some point, I learned that Lucha came to have a litter of puppies because a neighbor's dog had mounted her. Soon I saw that dogs everywhere investigated each other on meeting, and then one would jump onto the other. There was a process here, though I did not exactly understand it.

The farm also had a purebred bull donated by Heifer Project. He was fierce enough that he was kept inside an adobe enclosure behind the barn where he had stripped the bark from a tree. Dad hung an old tire from the tree for him to "play with," and that too was destroyed by his long, sharp horns. A ring in the bull's nose was used to control him when he needed to be moved into the breeding chute. The mission made the bull available to the local farmers so that they could improve their own herds by breeding their cows with the purebred bull.

When a farmer brought his cow to breed with the bull, the cow was led into a narrow stall or chute at the end of the barn. Once she was situated, the gate to the bull's pen was opened, and he was led by his nose ring into the same stall. The bull sniffed and licked the cow's rear, and then, resting his chin on her back, he raised up on his back legs, his front legs around the belly of the cow. After one or two quick thrusts, the bull backed down, leaving the cow with her tail to the side and a long, red organ hanging from the bull's belly.

My mother was shocked when she looked out the window and saw her little pigtailed girls, standing in their hand-knit sweaters with embroidered flowers, licking lollipops and watching the bull mount the cow. "Oh, Benton, you shouldn't let them watch!" But Dad grew up on a farm and saw no harm in it. We watched with the same interest that we watched the oxen plow a furrow or the hired man use a sickle to cut alfalfa. It was all just part of life in the countryside.

The naturalness of animals mating was so different from what we were to learn the morning Pedro, Mercedes's father, came to the house. When my sister and I came into the kitchen, Mom was already up, and the woodstove was hot. But the kitchen table was not set for breakfast. *Hurlbut's Story of the Bible* sat alone on the oilcloth table covering. We always read a story from this book after breakfast. This was no bland children's Bible. It chronicled the many macabre Old Testament stories in detail. I remember Mom laughing at phrases like, "He rides like Jehoshaphat," and "They flang down Jezebel." But some details were left out of even these stories, like the fact that Abraham was also the father of Ishmael. It just said, "Now there were two boys in Abraham's tent, the older boy, Ishmael, the son of Hagar, and the younger boy, Isaac, the son of Abraham and Sarah."

This morning, Mom was going have to tell us the rest of the story. She told us to sit down on the chairs beside the basement door. The kitchen was long with a window at one end, and at the other end, a door led into the laundry room, where Mom struggled with that washing machine. Between the laundry room and the kerosene refrigerator, a door led down to the basement. The cellar was cool, dark and musty, its steps used for storing things for easy access, like the wooden cases of Cokes we enjoyed on a Sunday and the baskets of eggs being collected for hatching. Two of the chairs that could be pulled up to the table for meals rested on either side of the cellar door, and now we sat down on the chairs. On the other side of the kitchen table, the door into the dining room and living room was closed. Through the door came the scent of damp wool ponchos and felt hats and the musky scent of anguished men. We could hear the low murmuring of men's voices. There was a confab going on on the other side of that door, and it didn't sound pleasant.

Mom took a deep breath and started.

"Last night, Manuel came home unexpectedly from Quito and found Pedro in bed with his wife Francisca. Instead of getting into a fight, they came here for help to figure things out," she explained.

Jan looked puzzled. "What is wrong with sleeping with someone else? Our friends sleep in our beds when they come to spend the night."

Mom struggled for words. "They were in bed as man and woman. God created male and female bodies to fit together like puzzle pieces. Sex is one of the ways people show love for each other when they are married. But Pedro and Francisca are not married. So they shouldn't have been in bed together."

We continued to look puzzled. She sighed. "When they are in bed together they lie side by side. That is how babies are made. Well, women have wombs where babies grow. They grow when the egg from the woman gets together with the sperm from the man."

"Okay?" I said, quizzically.

Then she described it right out!

"Eooh!" I said. "You mean Dad put (I couldn't say it) there before we were born?"

"Jeanne, don't say that," Jan begged. But Mom nodded.

"The thing is, sex can be a beautiful thing if it happens between married people who love each other." (I doubted that.) "But it is wrong outside of marriage," she said. And what had happened at Manuel's house was clearly wrong. Pedro was Mercedes's father, and she was my best friend, so this was serious. More importantly, her family members were leaders in the church, and Pedro was learning to be a pastor from my dad. He had been preaching every other Sunday and met with Dad regularly to study the Bible. In this case, though, it seems that he had made a pastoral call and just stayed over. Most of the men in the community worked in Quito during the week and came home on weekends, so he did not expect that Manuel would be coming home that night.

This was a turning point for Mercedes's family, and it was not a good one. I don't know what was said there in the living room, but Pedro's life seemed to descend into darkness after that day—or maybe it was after the night before. He never came back to church. He returned to his work of playing his harp at fiestas, being paid in chichi, the fermented corn beer. When he had joined the church, the missionaries had encouraged him to stop drinking and to play the harp in church instead. I never remember him playing the harp in church, and Mercedes says he never did. Instead, he played the harp at marriages, funerals, or other *fiestas*, and he drank himself into a stupor. Sometimes, when we drove past a fiesta, I could see the bow of his harp behind the bobbing hats and ponchos of drunken, dancing men, and I felt terrified and heartbroken.

Now, I stare at the tablecloth on the small wooden table in Mercedes's tiny dining room as we prepare to walk the entire community. Her house is smaller than her daughter's, with fewer windows. In the style of older homes, each room is separated from the others by a door, not the openness of Elizabeth's modern ranch-style house. But Mercedes has proudly shown me the fireplace at the end of the living room, a welcoming place on chilly evenings, not unlike the fireplace at the end of the living room of my childhood. The days are flying by so quickly; I have been here a week. There is much I still want to see. Before we go, we pause to talk over fruit smoothies and leftover tortillas. I am still thinking about how the situation with her father was handled after he "fell from Grace." I decide to ask.

"When he fell into adultery with a sister from the church, he was expelled from the church," she says. "My father was expelled."

"I remember the morning when they arrived at our house, your father with the woman's husband. I wonder what my father said," I say. "Do you think it was right, what the church did?"

"The word of God says that: not to be contaminated. We are supporters of that. But sometimes I wonder if it is right," she says. "It was so painful for us because he was left totally abandoned with his sin, totally abandoned."

"I do remember that," I nod, thinking of the broken, dejected look I recalled as he left our house that morning.

"He became violent. They did what the scriptures say. But I wonder if the others in the church could not have at least walked with him, as brothers, as family, as countrymen, if they could not have tried to restore this person. He was left completely abandoned," she says. "Even the larger community did not receive him. They had already rejected him because he was a believer."

I mention how Jesus says in Matthew 18 that when one member sins, first one person should go to him. And if he does not repent, the member should return with one or two others. Does that apply?

"But, my father did repent." She looks anguished. "On his knees, he begged the husband's pardon. He begged and begged, but the husband said he could not forgive. It's hard, isn't it? I don't fault the husband. It was especially hard because the couple continued to come to the church and my father would be there…"

As I moved into adolescence, my mother tried to caution me about "being careful." The violent image of dogs mounting other dogs or the bull mounting the small local cows might have sufficed. But for me, the image of sitting in the corner of the kitchen in the early morning cold, learning about sex as a destructive force gone out of control will always be the image I carry when I remember my introduction to sex and the impact it had on the community and people I loved.

Chapter 16
Pelicans Mate for Life

After Mercedes and I reflect on the sad story of her father, it crosses my mind that marriage does not solve all the problems of men and women together. I think of the pelicans I once saw on the beach in Ecuador. Unlike too many humans, pelicans are said to mate for life. For most, if not all, humans, it takes a lot of work (and a lot of fun) building a partnership that lasts a lifetime. As I watched this pair of pelicans, I learned about some of what it takes for both pelicans and humans to live out their commitment to their mates and to their families.

Someone, perhaps a doctor, had told the missionaries who worked in the high altitude of Ecuador that they should get out of the altitude once a year. Quito sits nine thousand feet above sea level, so we "had" to go on vacation either on the coast or into the Amazon jungle once a year. One of our favorite places for vacation was Playas, which means Beaches, along the southern coast of Ecuador. While these vacations may or may not have had physical health benefits, they certainly were beneficial to building of family relationships.

The family loaded suitcases on top of the red and silver GMC carry-all and all piled in. The GMC's top was painted silver because when it arrived in Ecuador painted all red, it was immediately impounded due to a rule that no one was allowed to drive an all-red vehicle except the fire chief. To get it released, Dad had to take it to a body shop and have the top part painted silver.

The drive to Playas started on the Pan-American Highway that ran through Quito, that cobblestone road that wound through the

Andes Mountains. When we passed through the highest altitudes, above the tree line, we drove through golden *páramo* grass and past low, grass-roofed houses. The people were short of stature and held their ponchos and shawls around them to ward off the cold, pulling their wide-brimmed white hats down over their faces. Fighting bulls were pastured in the páramo, so there were sometimes cowboys in sheepskin chaps, on horses, moving the bulls from one pasture to another. Once we met one of these bulls in the road. Two cowboys had lassos around the horns of the bull, but he was not so easily controlled, and as we edged our car past, the bull turned and charged the car, "goring" the passenger door and severing the handle. When we could move on, we did, not daring to stop and make any kind of claim.

At Ambato we left the high mountains and moved toward the coast. My dad recalled that he had gone to Ambato in 1949 to help with relief after a devastating earthquake leveled most of the area. He pointed out ravines that were actually large cracks in the land that had swallowed whole neighborhoods. We drove out a side road that ended abruptly at a drop-off into a valley. The rest of the road had disappeared in the earthquake. After several years, there were still people living in the central plaza in shelters made from woven mats, and we passed the ruins of a church where the arch over the altar was the only thing standing. He told us about how a group of girls were in a catechism class when the earthquake struck, and those under the arch were the only ones who survived. I pictured my father handing bags of food and blankets from the back of the truck to the desperate people and I felt proud.

Even as we left the Pan-American Highway and moved west toward the coast, the road continued to wind along the edges of mountainsides, with cliffs going straight up on one side and straight down on the other. The vegetation became greener and lusher, ferns and orchids clinging to the cliffs we passed. I knew that my mother loved both. I had tried many times in vain to get a fern that I found in the quebrada to grow in a tin can for her. But orchids did not grow near where we lived, so Dad decided to get one for Mom. He stopped the car on a narrow stretch of road where oncoming cars would have difficulty passing us. On one side was the rock wall, dripping with moisture, slippery with moss, ferns, and orchids clinging to loose rocks, and on the other side was a precipitous drop-off separated tentatively from the road by a few cactus plants. We looked out over treetops that grew on the canyon floor. More than once, I remember seeing the rusted bodies of vehicles that had missed a curve and plummeted down into the canyon. In front of us, the narrow cobblestone road curved around the side of the mountain, making us invisible to any oncoming cars or trucks.

"Oh, Benton," my mother said. "It is too dangerous. You might fall, and then what will we do? I don't NEED an orchid." But need and want are two different things, and vacation is about doing what you want to do. Dad got out of the car and climbed the side of the cliff, returning with a beautiful orchid for my mother. We kids looked on with wonder and awe.

As we moved out of the altitude, we started to see the tall trunks and top branches of kapok trees reaching up from the valley below. Pods with cottony fluff hung from the branches, their fluff used in mattresses and pillows. The beds where we would sleep that night would have the hard, heavy kapok pillows made from these trees.

Under their branches grew banana trees. At that time bananas were Ecuador's major export. Out from among flat green leaves the size of elephants' ears emerged long stems reaching out sensuously, and at the end of each stem hung a huge stalk of green bananas four to five feet long with the ends of the bananas all pointing upward. Below that, like the head of a phallus, hung the most amazing, huge purple heart-shaped flower. Like their lush vegetation, the lowland people also seemed to be more open, casual, and less modest than high in the Sierra where we lived.

We crossed a river at the town of Babahoyo, which I am told means "slime pit." The heat and humidity settled in oppressively. The town had no paved streets and few sidewalks, and the muddy streets had a stench of rotten fruit, decaying fish, and human and animal excrement. Turkey buzzards roamed freely. When Jan and I tried to chase them, Mom pulled us back. "They are filthy. This town has no garbage service, so it is illegal to disturb the buzzards because they keep the streets clean." The road ended at the river's edge and restarted on the other side. Connecting the two ends of road was a "bridge" made of balsa logs lashed together. Balsa is extremely buoyant, so the bridge floated on the surface of the river, but Dad was hesitant to drive out onto it with us in the car. So the family got out of the car and waited while he drove across, then crossed on foot, clutching each other's hands tightly.

We passed quickly through Guayaquil, the major port city of Ecuador, hot and humid, full of mosquitoes, vulgar language, and street fights. It held little more appeal for me than Babahoyo had. I watched in horror as a little boy cried while several men pummeled his father with their fists. We quickly moved on through the city and out the peninsula toward the coast, toward Playas, Beaches.

Most seaside resort towns at that time were little more than sleepy fishing villages with long, almost deserted beaches and a few small rooming houses across the street from the beach. But Playas boasted the majestic Humboldt Hotel, inaugurated in 1949 to the strains of the Costa Rican Swing Boys orchestra playing on one of the terraces. It had about forty guest rooms and boasted a heated saltwater pool and a romantic Spanish courtyard. We did not stay there, but Dad and I did walk around it early one morning when most of the guests were likely still sleeping off the previous evening's revelry. I was awed by the high stone walls that kept intruders and poor missionaries out.

The rooming house where we stayed was more modest than the Humboldt but luxurious compared to the thatched huts of the villagers. White tiles covered the floor and the steps on the main floor, and when we went upstairs we were pleased to see clean, fresh bedrooms with pressed cotton sheets and pillowcases over the firm kapok pillows. The owners of the house treated us like honored guests.

Meals were served in the large main room on pressed white tablecloths. Breakfast was always steaming cups of hot milk with shots of very strong coffee and lots of sugar, accompanied by hard French-style rolls and slices of salami and cheese. We tried to save money by picnicking at noon. Dinner in the evening often included *ceviche*, the traditional Ecuadorian seafood dish of shrimp marinated in lemon juice and hot sauce. Once they offered us raw oysters. My mother did not want to try them, but Dad and I did. I always wanted to try whatever Dad tried. The owner explained that the way to determine if an oyster is fresh is to squeeze lemon on it. If it moves, it is alive and, thus, fresh. I don't know which I liked better—the salty taste of the oysters or the bond of sharing an unusual liking with my father.

Dad and I liked to get up early, while my mother's idea of vacation was getting to sleep in, as much as vacationing with four small children would allow. We walked down the long beach, watching the fishermen guiding their rafts up onto the beach, each raft made of two or three balsa logs lashed together and a single sail. Two rafts worked together to pull a large net up onto the beach, where fish sellers were waiting and helped to pull the nets in when they had reached the shore. People crowded around the nets haggling over prices for the fish. Children also came with coconut shells to gather the unusual, non-edible catches. The first sea horse I ever saw was floating in a coconut shell on the beach, and I wanted to buy it from the boy, but my dad said it would not survive.

After breakfast, our family would take a picnic lunch, a beach blanket, inner tubes, and sand pails down to the beach. If we got thirsty, there was usually someone with a machete who would climb a palm tree and bring down a green coconut, then hack off one end and let us drink the refreshing coconut water. When we finished, he would chop the coconut in half, and we would use the piece he had hacked off earlier to scoop out the soft, milky flesh that most people would be familiar with as shredded coconut in grocery stores.

We picked up small, shiny shells, and Mom encouraged us to pick up enough to make necklaces, but when we brought them up to our room, they smelled of rotting fish. Dad suggested that we take them back out to the beach, and we laid them out on a piece of newspaper under a palm tree and left them there. After a few days, the ants had cleaned out the insides of the shells and we were able to bring them in and wash them, and after we got home, we strung them together into necklaces.

My parents became playful in this relaxed environment. Dad tried to climb a palm tree and bring down a coconut. He didn't make it to the top. Mom, in her black two-piece swimsuit, showed us how to scoop wet sand to make it look like a seashell. Then, while she lay in the sun on the blanket, we ran and frolicked in the warm

Pacific water or built castles in the sand and watched the incoming tide wash them away.

At the end of the beach, on the rocks, a pair of pelicans swooped into the water after fish. Their wide wings lifted their ungainly beaks as they came out of the water carrying their catch. Each day we watched them. When we kids tried to approach them, they would hurry away, always together. But as the days passed, we noticed that one was no longer flying and catching fish. She limped along the sand and her partner brought her food. Then, one day, we saw her lying on the rocks. Her partner paced around her, occasionally nudging her as if to urge her to get up. The buzzards soon took note and circled, waiting for her to die. After they began to feast on her flesh, her partner began to limp along the beach and then grew thinner, and it was clear that, in his grief, he was no longer feasting on fresh fish. By the time we left for home, the pelican partner had also died.

As I listened to Mercedes's stories of family violence, I wonder that these birds were able to care for each other all their lives, but the people of my Llano Grande community found it so difficult to do the same.

Andres and his chickens.

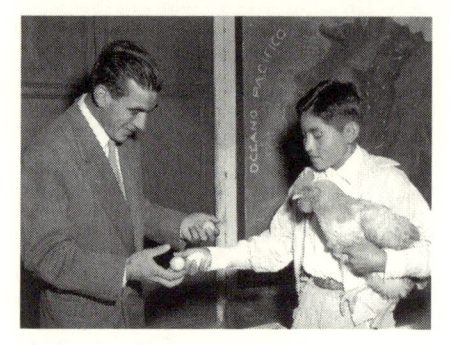

Andres presenting his eggs to one of the the teachers, Juan Benalcazar

Grandma, Orpha Rhoades, holding Becca, Paul Rhoades, Jeanne, Jan, Ruby, in front of the GMC carry-all.

Ruby at la playa, the beach. These were rare, treasured vacation times.

Chapter 17
Domestic Violence in the Town

Household tasks finished, Mercedes says we should be leaving while the morning is still cool. We take a long walk through the community and end up at the home of Mercedes's brother Enrique and his wife Laura. We talk for quite a while, catching up on their lives and getting to know Enrique's wife and family. Laura is a small woman with long black hair and the heavy features typical of indigenous women, but her smile crinkles her face. Mercedes counts Laura as her strongest ally against domestic violence. I know that she and Enrique were youthful sweethearts and their closeness is still evident in the work they do together in their garden and home and in the stories she and Enrique share about their life together. I'm concentrating, as always on this visit, on the changing customs in my old home village. Because I am interested in marriage particularly and have been thinking about it a lot, including the sad story of Pedro's infidelity, I've asked pointed questions about its customs. Mercedes has told me he is the one to talk about this.

Enrique tells me that when he and Laura were married, they had both a church wedding, in the evangelical church, and a native wedding. I ask him what that native wedding was like. "Well, in the first place, the groom's parents are required, the groom's parents with his whole family have to go and ask the lady. You can go with music, you can go with harp, drum, *viandas*."

I ask, "Vianda, what is that?"

"Vianda, lots of things to eat. There would be fruits, cereals, live birds, dead birds. They would have to carry baskets with each of these, with bread and cuyes, guinea pigs. The woman's parents first ask, 'How have you been?' When the young man asks to marry their daughter, the woman's family at first objects. But the groom insists, he insists even past midnight. Finally, her parents say 'Good, okay you can marry.' This is a very rich prelude. It is a kind of negotiation among the elders after the young are already committed. And once accepted, it is the job of the parents and the couple to get a sponsor, a *padrina* couple."

"Godparents…" I fill in.

"Yes, godparents, who must be older and of good conduct. Once you seek the godfather, the godfather does not accept immediately, right? He always refuses a little, and says it is a very big responsibility. But finally he has to accept. Then, they choose the church. In our case this was a problem because the godparents were not from the evangelical church and even so, could object to being godparents, once the decision is already made. The couple now decides what church, what place, what time, and what you need do. The Catholic Church has a practice called *flokama*, a 'kichwised' word for proclamation, saying that two people are getting married. The next six days or so, in colonial times, were used to abuse the bride. The priests would abuse the bride, with the pretext of proclaiming the nuptials."

"What?" I ask, astonished.

"Historically, this horror was called *pernada*; the feudal right of the land owner, the sheriff, and the priest to take advantage of the bride before her marriage. For that reason, we preferred the evangelical church where they don't put a hand on anyone; they respect people. Once the church has agreed to the event, all the preparations begin in the family and community. Each family contributes something so they can have chickens, a pig, pumpkin, corn, potatoes, peas. It becomes a minga for all. The godfather would give them a piece of land, and everyone helped to build a house. Now we no longer do that, but we still have contributions of foods, beverages, and preparation of clothes. Once you are ready with the clothes and all that, then you meet your church obligations and return home. That is when the community celebration begins, that is where people come with a *maltas* of chichi; a *malta* is the vessel that, you know, is carried on the shoulder."

"I do remember the large clay jars." Enrique has paused to watch his young adult daughter enter the room and sit down on the sofa across from us. I wonder if she has heard this story before.

"They bring liquor or beer. Or it may be that they bring *pucayos*, which are foods like roasted meats, things like *mote* or hominy, to give to the family."

"And bread." Mercedes adds. She has put down her hat and water bottle and is listening intently. I think they are pleased someone is asking in detail about the old customs in this age where they are disappearing.

"Bread, especially bread, always, right? Always great loaves of bread. While they bring these things, a ceremony begins at the home. First of all, they ask the blessing of parents of the bride and the groom's parents. After the blessing of the family, the couple is given advice, such as, 'you have to behave yourself,' and everything else. Then they tie the man and the woman with a *chumbi*, a woven belt. Two women take the man and two men carry the woman, and they race from the groom's house to the bride's house. This is called, it is called *jayuna tantan*."

"*Kiroaisi*," Mercedes corrects him with a wink.

"Kiroaisi, right. The music they play is the jayuna tantan. But the kiroaisana, it's like a man or woman having to carry a heavy piece of wood and having to run from the groom's house to the house of the bride. The person who finishes first wins and gets a prize of a malta of chicha and a basket of mote, hominy, for their family. In my case I won, in spite of being behind. Although the women were good runners, they had trouble carrying me. And the men had trouble with Laura because they had to go over ditches and other obstacles. When you reach the house, you have to kneel for the whole family to tell on you, secrets to reveal during this marriage ceremony. Some will say that you have been rude, bad, or very drunk, too lazy and not a hard worker. Others, however, cry because they don't want to be separated, the sisters especially cry and the close family members. Finally, there is another huge meal with lots of music. The music tells what time it is in the ceremony. The drum and trumpet announce if they are in the blessing, or kiroaisana, or already eating, or some other activity, in my case opening gifts. When it's getting late, the music of the band lets people know it is the final ceremony of the night." He turns to Mercedes. "What is the name of that, Ñañita [little sister]? What did the band play?"

"It's called *mashalla*."

"Yes, mashalla. They are in the house of the bride and make a song specifically for the son-in-law. There has to be the band, the drum, and there must be a man singing. There are fifty-seven verses. The bride and groom are in the middle, close relatives are around dancing and singing mashalla. The verses are all advice. 'If the husband comes from work tired, you have to feed him, treat him well and the husband has to find a way to get the means to survive.' All these tips have been practiced for many years. Until today that is done. Once this is finished, the couple are caught by the godparents and taken to their home and locked in. This happens on the wedding night, instead of the honeymoon in Acapulco you see today." We all smile.

"On the wedding night, in our case someone was stationed outside our door so that we couldn't escape. That person at the door was to be punished if we escaped. Of course, we were super-exhausted and just slept. The next day, in these weddings, the godfather does *ataich*, which means raising the couple up with the drum, music, and everything else, like food. Then the band goes to the godfather's home. All this ends Tuesday or Wednesday, having begun between Saturday and Sunday. That is the end of food, dancing, singing performances, people taking the floor to speak." He stops and shrugs. "That's a native marriage. Much is spent on orchestra, band, music. But it doesn't compare to the modern wedding." He sighs, remembering.

We visit a while longer and say goodbye, and as Mercedes and I head home, I reflect on what I have known over the years about Ecuadorian life between men and women. Enrique has been speaking about wedding customs, but what about the marriage, the give and take that keeps it working over a lifetime? Even as a young child, I was aware of the violence men in Llano Grande and throughout Ecuador inflicted on each other and on their wives. It keeps recurring in these stories about the Ecuadorian countryside. It was how I got an unwished-for lesson on how the sexes interact, that day in our kitchen, but every week it could be seen right out on the road.

Our family rarely traveled into the community on Sunday afternoons. To leave the farm, it was necessary to pass Cuatro Esquinas, Four Corners. On that corner was the chicharia, or saloon. At one side of the low adobe building was a volleyball court. Sunday afternoons, the men would gather there to play and to quench their thirst with chicha. Then their wives—if these women were still sober—or their children would be responsible for helping them get home.

Often, the drunken adult was not able to get home and fell at the side of the road. If we did go out on Sunday afternoon, we were sure to pass a number of adults crumpled in the ditch with their children sitting beside them, covering them with their ponchos or shawls to keep off the dust or rain and trying to make sure they were not robbed.

What frightened me most was the fighting. Men would fight with each other or beat their wives right there on the road. One afternoon, as we drove down the dusty, narrow road, we had to slow to avoid two men who were fighting in the middle of the road. The men separated briefly to let us pass, but as we eased our way through, one of the men came up to the car. I watched in horror, unable to turn away, as he pressed his battered, bloody face up to the car window beside me. After that, I frequently woke up with nightmares of being chased by a drunken, bleeding man.

One Sunday afternoon, we were invited to the home of one of the church members. It was at the far end of Llano Grande where the road was little more than a footpath. As we left their house, we passed a man beating his wife at the side of the road. The woman's shawl lay at her feet. The man grabbed the front of her embroidered blouse and pounded her face. A little child clutched at her skirt, crying, while a baby bounced back and forth on her back. I am sure my father wanted to intervene and might have if he did not have his whole family in the car. I believe that later he did speak to the man about his drunken behavior and the man expressed his shame, but the drunkenness and violence continued.

"And now you are doing something about the violence," I say to Mercedes.

"Yes," she answers, her face resolute. "But it has been like pushing a huge boulder up a hill." She tells me about her mother-in-law. This woman and her young son Alfredo came to live with the newly married Andrés and Mercedes after Andrés Sr. left her for a younger woman, a woman the age of his own son.

"Her hands were crippled and almost useless. The fingers had been broken so many times. When she showed me her head, there were places where the hair didn't grow. Her scalp was so scarred from having her hair pulled out."

I nod. "I know. My father was called more than once to try to stop your father-in-law. He told us about getting to the house and finding your mother-in-law tied to a post by her hair while Andrés Sr. beat her face."

"My own Andrés has told me about coming to get your father when he was afraid his father would kill his mother," she says. "Andrés's younger brother Alfredo has been so bitter about all that. When his mother died in the bus accident, people all came around to offer his father comfort. But, I ask, where were they when his father was beating and mistreating his mother?"

That family had so much tragedy. I remember when Andrés's little sister was tragically killed by a speeding car. His mother had taken a basket of mote to Quito to sell. She regularly made mote, just as Mercedes's mother made humitas, to sell on the streets of Quito. She had taken several of her small children with her. As she sat on the street corner with the mote, the children ran about nearby. The little girl ran out into the street and was struck by a passing car.

My mother went to the home to offer comfort at that time. When she returned, she sank into the kitchen chair, silently shaking her head. "It was heartbreaking. The house was filled with mourners, crying and chanting. The mother sat in a corner wailing, '*Mi chiquita, mi negrita, mi chanchita,* my little one, my little black one, my small piglet.'" I thought those were strange things to be saying, but Mom told me that they were all terms of endearment for indigenous people.

She sighed. "And where was Andrés Sr.? You would think he would be there to comfort her. No, he went to the chicharia with some other men. He will probably come home drunk and beat her for letting this happen to their daughter." And so it went.

Andrés Sr. was one of the more prosperous members of the community. He owned property up in the fertile Guayllabamba Valley where he grew avocados and *chirimoyas*, or custard apples. While most men in the community worked all week in Quito as gardeners, houseboys, or street sweepers, he was able to prosper as a fruit merchant. When he was sober, he assumed leadership in the church and community, but when he had been drinking, he became particularly violent. How could his son grow up to be any different? I wondered. How much would Mercedes be willing to confide about her husband now, with our reawakening friendship? There was no question but that we had reconnected over our shared memories, but I knew her own husband had been at times like his father. Would she tell me?

I remember her Andrés as a child, being one of the more outstanding kids in the school and church. When the mission distributed Heifer Project chickens to the schoolchildren, he was the first to get a chicken house built beside his home. His chickens did so well that he and his father soon developed a thriving business raising and dressing chickens to sell in Quito, a business that he maintained well into adulthood.

> **From my Dad's letter home:**
> *May 1956*
> *Dear folks,*
> *...Last Sunday we distributed some 140 chickens here in the community. Earlier, 150 were distributed from here to other 4H clubs of the area by US Point IV. Both they and Heifer Project cooperate with us in this project. We are only in charge of raising the chicks from 3 days to six weeks of age and distributing in this community. We get our cost out of it which this time was 9 sucres or 56 cents apiece, and believe we are doing a lot of the families a good turn as well as making some good contacts both with government and with other rural schools... The next shipment of 500 will arrive May 28 and I hope I can be ready for them...*
> *Love, Benton*

I remember going to the airport to pick up that shipment of chicks. They traveled on a cargo plane that was not heated, so they came in the cockpit with the pilots. Dad drove the pickup truck out onto the runway where the plane had landed. The pilot greeted us and handed down boxes of day-old chicks. The cardboard boxes with little holes were stacked in the cab of the truck to keep the chicks warm, and tiny, fuzzy yellow heads poked out through the holes in the box. At the farm a brooder house had been prepared with a kerosene heater to keep the chicks warm until they were big enough to be distributed to the schoolchildren. Llano Grande was close enough to Quito to get dressed chickens quickly to market, so the chickens provided a strong source of income for the people for many years and, for Andres, the promise of a good livelihood.

We have come back to Mercedes's comfortable house and sit on the steps outside her kitchen door. Not much remains from the former chicken sheds that once housed a flourishing poultry business. Grandson Ernesto's soccer goal now sits on the bare and cracked concrete floors. Still, they raise chickens, free range. Hens scratch in the dirt path that joins her house to Elizabeth's. Outside the gate that surrounds both houses, a semi rumbles past, stirring up a cloud of dust. Mercedes frowns and reaches out to pat the head of one of her watchdogs, who has come to visit us.

She tells me that she married Andrés after finishing college and spending a year teaching native children in the jungle. Andrés had promised she would be able to continue her beloved career as a teacher, but shortly after they married, he insisted that she leave her work and devote herself exclusively to being a wife and mother. And he was unnecessarily demanding, macho. "When he was driving up to the house, he would blow the horn loud and expect me to have dinner ready the moment he walked in the door."

I'm not sure what caused the women of the community to rise up, but rise up they did, Mercedes among the first. Perhaps, it was their education and increasing prosperity. Or, maybe they had just had enough. Mercedes tells me, "For me, the turning point came a number of years into our marriage with my illness. I had severe stomach pain and headaches. I couldn't move one of my arms. Andrés had borrowed money to invest in new equipment for dressing the poultry, but the business was failing. Then I learned that he had fathered a child with another woman. I lost the will to live.

"That is when my daughter Elizabeth came back to visit from Spain, where she was living at the time. She was shocked to see me, and she cut her visit short to take me back to Spain with her. I went to many doctors, but they could not find anything physically wrong. Finally, one recommended that I see a psychiatrist. He really understood, telling me that I should first forgive myself, then forgive others, and finally let go of the things I could not control. I knew that the relationship with Andrés was something I could control, so I came home and clearly told him that he must stop abusing me or I would leave."

She says the abuse has stopped. Still, I do not see the warmth in their relationship that I see in that of her daughter Elizabeth and Elizabeth's husband Fabian. They enjoy working together in the kitchen and going together to watch their son Ernesto play soccer. Fabian sits close to Elizabeth at meals and frequently smiles and winks at her during conversations.

The other dog nuzzles his way past the first for an affectionate scratch behind his ear. Mercedes continues. "After I saw that women could have some control over their lives, I began to talk with other women in the community. Finally, we decided to have a march against domestic violence. We made placards and gathered at one end of the village, then we marched to the other end. As we passed homes, we invited the women to come out and join us. The march grew bigger as we went along. As we drew to the end, women began marching right back into their own houses and bringing their husbands out to publically denounce them for their abuse.

"When I left that morning, Andrés slapped me and said, 'This is what I think of your march.' But that just gave me more reason to march. At the end of the march, one woman said, 'I was so afraid to join you. I hoped that no one would recognize me. Every house we passed, I had to fight the urge to disappear inside.' But," Mercedes smiles, "when we got to her house, she marched right in and brought her husband out to denounce him."

I ask what the outcome has been. She tells me that many men

have changed their ways. The wives of those who would not change have left the marriages. Later on, when I am in Quito, I ask a missionary friend who teaches family therapists about the change. "It's true," she says. "There has been a nationwide campaign against domestic violence. It is amazing that the situation could change in just one generation."

Chapter 18
Walking with Dad

I have always loved to walk. During my time in Llano Grande, in addition to the sheer enjoyment of it, walking gives me the chance to get close to all of the sights, sounds, and even smells that take me back to the childhood home I yearn to touch. I savor every moment of feeling the sunshine beating down on my arms, every little flower peeking up through the hard earth, the feel of dust and pebbles under my feet, the scent of food being cooked by roadside vendors, the shouts of children and barking of dogs.

I've been here over a week now. Today, after last evening's talk on the steps outside Mercedes's house, taking a long morning walk with my friend gives me the added pleasure of seeing some of the community through her eyes as we stop to talk with people she has known since her childhood. She pauses to introduce them to me and to remind me that I may have known them long ago, perhaps even carried one or two on my back when I was a child and they were babies. Some I seem to recall; most not.

As Mercedes and I stop at the sidewalk table of a small grocery for a bottle of cold mineral water, I silently gaze down the road ahead. I remember walking behind my dad, along the dusty paths in Llano Grande so many years ago, carefully placing my feet into the prints his shoes left in the dust of the road. People seemed to know him, nodding and saying "…Dias." I copied his reply of "…Dias" to them with the same nod of the head. I was in first grade, home from boarding school, and got to go "visiting" with my dad. We spent the day walking through the community of Llano Grande, stopping to talk with people along the road, in the fields, or in front of their homes. While he talked, I explored the small plot of land where a family lived. There was usually a tree—chickens liked to roost there—and there was a pit where the rabbits lived. The rabbits made little burrows along the bottom of the pit; weeds and crop scraps were thrown in to feed them. Dad liked to stand with a foot up on the porch ledge and chew on a bit of grass while they talked. Some folks would offer us a little food, a soft-boiled egg or a tangerine.

In Dad's memoirs, he recalls one home that especially welcomed him. "Maria T (Tia Maria), a sensitive Quechua Indian woman invited me into her house, her family life, her own soul when I felt foreign, alien, feared and rejected by the people whom I wanted to know and serve. Walking on the dusty road in the hot Equatorial sun in Llano Grande, dry and thirsty and alone—Maria invited me in to sit beside the adobe casa in the shade to talk, to listen to her story, to tell her mine." That was, of course, Mercedes's mom.

At noon, Dad and I stopped under a line of cypress trees and shared our lunch. I don't remember what we ate, though I did appreciate the refreshing thermos of water on the dusty, dry day. He talked about who else we would be visiting that day.

"We will be stopping to see Pedro and Segundo's mother," Dad said.

"I know them," I told him, looking up into his face. "Will they be at home? Can I play with them while you talk with their mother?"

"No, they are in school today. But you will enjoy their mother. She is always laughing."

We got to the little adobe house with a thatched roof. Mrs. Muzo hobbled out onto the porch, leaning on a homemade crutch. Sometime in the past, her husband had dislocated her hip while beating her in a drunken rage. Now, she always needed to walk with the crutch.

Dad shook her hand. "*Buenas tardes.* Good afternoon, Mrs. Muzo. How are you? How is your family? Your mother and father; your children?" It would be rude to launch into his business without first asking about her health and her family.

Mrs. Muzo laughed. "So-so, Sr. Bentonsito. And how is your

family? La Sra. Ruby?" Fine, he said, then he got down to business.

"Today, I came to tell you about your doctor visit. I have the x-rays they took of your hip." He pulled the grey and black transparent film from his bag. "This is a picture of it—your hip."

She looked at the film and shook her head. "That is my hip?" She threw back her head, her shawl falling off of her hair, revealing the single braid wrapped in a red and black woven *faja*, and she laughed. She laughed until tears flowed and she nearly fell over.

Dad took the sprig of grass from his teeth and smiled. "The doctor thinks he can fix your hip with an operation in the hospital."

"The hospital," she said. "That is where my brother-in-law died last year. I won't go to the hospital. Never!"

Dad started to object, but her husband came out of the house. Then the husband told us, "Like she said, no operation. Things are all right as they are."

Dad put the x-ray back into his bag, and we again shook hands all around. As we walked away, he looked ahead, down the road. "It is so hard for people to change. Centuries of peonage and of being regarded as little better than beasts of burden as well as fear of outsiders make the people slow to respond." I was too young to fully understand his words, but I knew that he respected both the local people and me by the way that he talked.

Like Dad, I was the oldest child in the family and, like Dad, I tried to be the good child. I desperately wanted his approval all my life. And, I suppose I thought I might earn it by being like him. At that time, only a few courageous women were venturing into professions that were dominated by men, like pastoral ministry. The closest I might get to that would be to marry a minister, and that would require a whole other set of skills that had nothing to do with being like Dad. Later, when I was in high school, I did particularly well in chemistry, better, in fact, than some of the boys in my class who hoped to become doctors. So, I discussed with Dad the possibility of my studying medicine. He said, "I could picture myself being married to a nurse. But I can't imagine being married to a doctor." Since I did hope to marry, I chose to study nursing—a choice that I have never regretted in spite of the reason I made it.

Being like Dad and earning his approval became somewhat of

a moving target.

When my book club read and discussed *The Poisonwood Bible*, I commented, "It takes a kind of arrogance to travel to another country to tell people that you believe something they need to believe." I look at the picture of my parents and me boarding the plane for Ecuador in 1946. What thoughts and dreams were filling that young man's head as he left his home country for a perilous flight into the Andes Mountains with his baby daughter and pregnant wife to a country about which he knew so little? I wish I could ask him. But I doubt that he would be able to say.

Search of the Church of the Brethren archives revealed correspondence between my father and the Foreign Missions Commission early in his college years. Initially, he was interested in going to China. In June 1942, he wrote, "Dear Leland, You will remember the Committee Meeting at Camp Largo this past winter when Naylor and Austin were assigned to England for foreign relief service. At that time I also expressed my willingness to enter such service or any other type of work which the Brethren Service Committee saw fit. At that time you recommended to me that I finish my senior year at Manchester....I believe that I have an application on file with you. But, in case I do not, I will tell you something of myself and my work of the past few years. I am past 22 years old now and graduated from Manchester this year." I also learned that Dad had some hesitation about going to a country that was nominally Catholic. "A factor that might be mentioned is my lack thus far of any clearly defined philosophy of Protestant missions in a Catholic land. Of course, I realize that this philosophy will have to be partly evolved as we work at the job."

As his thinking evolved over the years, he seemed to forget who he had been earlier in life. Perhaps that was necessary for him to always be so sure that he knew the truth, even as that truth evolved for him. When I reminded him on the thirtieth anniversary of JFK's assassination that he had voted for Nixon, he forcefully denied it.

"You were against Kennedy because he was Catholic," I replied.

"Oh, no! I couldn't have... But, maybe I did."

By then, Dad had left behind the task of bring the "good news" to the nominally Catholic people (actually dominated by the medieval form of Catholicism) who we encountered when we went to Ecuador. Now, embracing the new ideas he saw as Catholicism seemed to evolve, he worked with ecumenical groups that included Roman Catholic teachers of liberation theology. Dad liked to identify himself as "the son of a landless farmer" and connected with the struggles of the poor and landless peasants throughout the world. Liberation theology seeks not only to serve the poor, but also to ask why they are poor. Based on the teachings of Jesus, it critiques the unjust economic, political, or social conditions that conspire to keep some people poor while the people in power profit. Dad became a master of this analysis.

Dad's progression in thinking reminded me of the fictional character of David Treadup in the novel *The Call* by John Hersey. It tells the story of a young missionary who went to China, full of a passion to share the gospel. Over the years, both China and the young missionary changed profoundly. After reading this novel, I gave Dad a copy. In the front, I wrote the following: "To the young man in the Zoot suit, boarding the plane with his wife and baby on his first trip to Ecuador and to the man he has become. I hope that you will someday learn to love them both as I do." I don't know if he ever read the book. He never told me. Nor do I know if he ever was able to love the young man who first heard the call to mission work. I wish he could have; both were good people and both accomplished important work.

I do know that, just before Dad's death, he returned to Ecuador with my nephew Nate, his grandson. He came to join a protest march against the Free Trade Area of the Americas that would be so damaging to the native peoples of Ecuador. During that trip, he met with the elders of Llano Grande one evening and asked their forgiveness. Now, on my visit, when they recall that evening to me, people shake their heads and ask, "Why? What is there to forgive when our lives are better because he came so many years ago?" Mercedes even tells me that her life was spared by the coming of the missionaries: "When I was a child, my belly was bloated with parasites, and your father came and brought medicine that saved me."

Nate commented on my dad's evolution in attitude at Dad's memorial service: "One of the most moving moments in my entire life was sitting in the dark little sanctuary in Llano Grande and watching as Grandpa gracefully and humbly asked forgiveness for having come there as a young, idealistic, white American missionary without having fully understood the power and privilege that afforded him. And watching, then, as several of the old grey-haired elders sat listening and nodding slowly in complete understanding, complete forgiveness, and complete love."

During my high school and college years, Dad worked for an ecumenical organization that provided technical support to rural missionaries throughout the world. Mom was working for a religious publishing company but went on to be the first woman executive in the Church of the Brethren, directing the World Ministries Commission.

I graduated from nursing school at a tumultuous time for the United States. Dr. Martin Luther King Jr. was killed that spring, days before I started my public health rotation in East Harlem, and Robert Kennedy was shot the night before my graduation. I felt an urgency to make a difference in the world, and Dad heartily supported that. I also hoped to test whether I might be called to mission work. I applied and was accepted to volunteer with the Mennonite Central Committee for two years.

Why did I choose the Mennonites since I was from the Church of the Brethren? In Dad's work, he often returned from trips overseas with stories about workers he had met in various countries. "Those young Mennonite men are right out there on the front lines, working with the people." He certainly admired them. So, I figured that those were the young men I would like to work with.

I was placed in northeast Brazil, at that time considered to be one of the neediest places in the world. We were the first volunteers from that organization to be sent there, and our start was difficult and confusing, particularly since we were all just out of college. At that time, the Latin American Catholic Church was experiencing an "awakening" in its call to serve and to stand with the poor. The official residence of the archbishop of Recife and Olinda was just down the street from the school where the other single female volunteer and I boarded. We were aware of their work with the poor and that other priests were working in the slums of the city. I had even met one who was running a clinic in one of the communities where I visited a former patient from the hospital. When I tried to engage him in conversation about how we might work together, he seemed to be avoiding my questions and indicated that I should not draw attention to his work. Of course, he had no idea if I was really a volunteer nurse or if I was working for my government in some kind of covert spying operation. The U.S. State Department was known to keep an eye on groups that worked with the poorest of the poor; they were suspected of being Communist. Dom Helder Camara, Archbishop of Recife and Olinda, said, "When I give food to the poor, they call me a saint; when I ask why the poor have no food, they say I am a communist."

Dad came to visit while I was there. He was traveling with a colleague who had worked as a nun in that part of the world. In his professional capacity, he met with the archbishop, among others. I tried to share with him our struggles finding our roles in this new land. But he seemed to be more interested in why we were not doing the kind of work the Catholics were doing. When I tried to explain, he said, "But you could at least be meeting with these radical young priests for Bible study and prayer." His criticism stung me in a way that can still bring tears to my eyes. I wanted so much to be understood, and instead I felt judged on a metric that I couldn't even understand.

Many years later, at a women's spiritual retreat, a priest led us through a meditation/visualization exercise. "Close your eyes and picture someone who has wounded you deeply…" I pictured Dad, whose approval I had so wanted and from whom I seemed to experience only disappointment. "Now, visualize that person walking toward you from a distance," the priest said. "As that person approaches, you move toward the person… When the person comes clearly into view, you see that it is your own wounded self… You reach out your arms and embrace that person… And you say, 'I forgive you.'"

I forgive you. Somehow, being able to forgive myself for how I had failed to be what I thought Dad wanted me to be removed the sting from my relationship with him. I felt some relief from the need to be like him or to be who I thought he thought I should be. But, still, I walk behind him, trying to put my feet into his footprints. It's just that now I do it in my own way.

Chapter 19
The Meaning of Land

My time in Llano Grande is nearing its end. On this, my next to last day, Mercedes and I walk down the road for a return visit to Enrique's home. He and Mercedes seem to share a special bond as brother and sister, not unlike my bond with my younger brother. Often when Enrique talks with her, he lapses into Kichwa, referring to her as ñañita, little sister, though she is the oldest. First we spend a few minutes sitting on the porch of Tia Maria's little house across the yard from Enrique's. Hers is a windowless, two-room house that Enrique built for her when her children thought it was no longer safe for her to continue living with their father, the fallen Pedro. One room contains her bed; the other has a small woodstove and a table and chair. A collage of old photographs on her bedroom wall includes a picture of her and Pedro as young people, and there is also a picture of my mother—the same picture that sits on my dresser at home. Tia Maria spends much of her day on the porch, selling things like humitas and boiled *habas*, fava beans, to passers-by.

I have some questions for Enrique, who seems to have perspectives about the past and also the present and future of his culture. Some things in my memory of our life here seem odd, unexplained. Perhaps Enrique can help me to understand.

I remember sitting in a smoky, windowless hut with Jan, when we were about six years old, while people outside gathered around Dad. Someone brought us a bowl of soup to eat. The soup had bits of chicken, actually a chicken foot, pieces of potato, and chunks of corn on the cob. There were also gourds of unfermented chicha. Not really understanding what was happening, we sipped the soup. Then we peeked through a crack in the door of the hut.

Men in ponchos and women in wool skirts and shawls were gathered around Dad, shouting. They had put a poncho on him and had him up on a horse. On the poncho, they had fastened live chickens, ears of corn, pineapples, and ripe papayas. They were beating drums, drinking, and dancing. Men drinking chichi always struck fear in me, so we just watched through the crack in the door.

Now, so many years later, I still don't really understand what was happening. So I ask Enrique. What was all that about? We are sitting in the dimly lit living room of his adobe house. Unlike Elizabeth's modern ranch-style house, where I am staying, Enrique's house has exposed beams, beyond which you can see the tile roof. Instead of carpets, his floor has esteras. On the walls hang pictures celebrating native culture, including a framed magazine cover picturing him as a much younger man with his wife Laura, both in native clothing. A native drum and guitar lean against the wall. Enrique has both feet and his heart firmly planted in the culture of his native land.

Outside, Enrique and Laura have cultivated an orchard of guava and lemon trees. Enrique sells lemons to juice bars in Quito. Mercedes says they had planted the orchard when they were experiencing persecution for their actions for indigenous rights, in case they couldn't find work. Enrique offers us guavas to eat. Earlier he took us back to see their pigs. The three pigs, each with a name, live in a moveable pen so they can eat the weeds and fertilize the soil with their excrement. Enrique moves the pen to another area of the orchard when the pigs have done their work.

As we sit in the living room, enjoying the guavas, Enrique answers the question that has puzzled me all my life. "Well," he says. "I know of that Andean ritual, the *jaichiwa*. It was practiced on the haciendas when the sharecroppers expressed thanks to the patrón, or landlord. It was a disgraceful throwback to the era of *latifundia*, the feudal landowner system that followed colonialism. It was the custom, after eight whole days of harvesting, when the patrón's barn was filled, to gather the best ears of corn and sew them onto a huge poncho and to go looking for the patrón. The patrón would be waiting with an enormous jar of liquor, and the people would put the poncho on him and oblige him to dance. They also expected the wife to dance, bearing a load of fruit. They always referred to the *patrona* as *niña* or 'little girl,' even if she was eighty or ninety years old. It was a form of domination on the part of the landowner, an abusive custom because all the patrón gave them for their hard work was liquor."

"I know that my father did not give them liquor," I say. "I know that the whole thing was embarrassing for him. And I'm sure that he did not dance, nor did my mother."

"I'm sure that Señora Ruby did not dance," Enrique says. "The missionaries didn't want us to dance. They said it was a sin. I don't understand that opinion of dancing, and I have told them so. It was robbing us of something so central to our culture. But most of the missionaries get defensive when I say this." I am told that Laura and Enrique's daughters have formed a folkloric dance troupe that performs in the city almost every weekend.

It seems the missionary effort, no matter how well intentioned, made other mistakes. Mercedes adds that once a missionary poured chicha on the ground when it was brought to express thanks for the opportunity to participate in planting crops. "I understand that the missionaries wanted to save the people from drunkenness, but pouring chichi on the ground was a great insult to the people. The missionaries did not understand that the indigenous people and the land are one and the same. If you ask them to leave the land and move somewhere else, the person who was born on the land will not leave. A person would die on his land; he is one with this land. Perhaps, the others who come later, who have not planted, have not weeded, for example, the youth of these times may not feel that unity. Still, you cannot insult the ground we live on."

When the Church of the Brethren started mission work in Ecuador, it was their desire to minister to the "whole person." They provided medical care, started a school, and demonstrated more progressive agriculture methods. The base for all of these efforts was the *hacienda* that the mission purchased. It was the era when foreign missions purchased land and established mission compounds throughout the developing world. In Llano Grande, the homes of the missionaries were separate from the hacienda that housed the school and church. It was never referred to as a compound.

From a survey done shortly after we arrived in Ecuador, I learn more about the choice of a community and property from which to start the mission work. Regarding Llano Grande, the missionaries found "…almost total illiteracy and lack of sanitation in the area. There is need for introduction of new dryland and irrigated crops, also home industries to supplement the income from the small plots on which they live. The majority of men now work in Quito as gardeners and street-cleaners. There is need for community recreation to take the place of the drunken fiestas. There is need for medical care. Most of all we see the need for the Church there."

Regarding land, they found "…land is extremely hard to obtain. The Indian is land-hungry and grasps, for a home, every small plot that is for sale. Some very large haciendas, ranging from hundreds to thousands of acres, are sometimes offered for sale. But, we do not believe that the church is interested either in such large operations or in real estate parcelization. Therefore, we are watching for a plot of 15–30 acres near an Indian village."

Until a professional agronomist arrived, Dad put his own experience as the son of a farmer to work on the land. But it was a large property, and he needed help from the local people. Before land reform, when a hacienda was sold, the sharecroppers or *huasipungueros* on the land came with the hacienda. So, the people who lived there stayed on and worked the land while the mission helped them with farming techniques. It had a sort of feudal feel that for the son of a tenant farmer was not a comfortable relationship. But neither would it be right to evict the people from the land.

Everywhere I go in Llano Grande, people also remember Señor Rolando, the missionary agronomist, who lived with his family near our own home. "He taught us how to raise better crops."

> **Rolland F, the agronomist, father of my friends Jim and John, described his work in the *Gospel Messenger* in 1953:**
>
> The dream, or obsession of every Andean Indian is land, a piece of land that he can call his very own. This possession of land gives the Indian a sense of security and a feeling of independence from the

white man. Ever since the coming of the Spanish, the Indians have been the laborers for the well-to-do, often absentee, hacienda owners. A hacienda is a big ranch or farm varying in size from a few hundred acres to as much as a thousand acres or more. The Indian was almost a slave, being sold along with the land if the land changed ownership.

Often the patron or owner would give each Indian worker about an acre of land on which to raise corn for his family and to build a mud shack with a straw roof. The Indian worked for the hacienda four or five days each week and the rest of the time could work on his own little plot.

Since we live near the capital city of Quito, most of the men of our community work there as street sweepers, gardeners, house servants or construction workers for contractors. For this reason the women do much of the farming, for the men come home once every two weeks or, if they are lucky, every Saturday evening and Sunday. Because the men are able to supplement the farm income with their wages earned in Quito, by careful economy—many are able to buy two or three acres of land and in this little area where we live almost seventy-five per cent of the Indians own a small plot of land. Some families rent land, the renter furnishing his own seed, tools and work, and giving half of the crops to the owner as rent; rarely ever is the land rented for cash.

One of our major concerns is to work toward crop improvement so that a few more men might be able to earn a comfortable living by working at home full time. Family life is difficult when the husband is away from home so much and it is not easy to maintain the Christian moral standards that we are striving for in such an unnatural separation of families.

The soil of this area needs building up and with all our modern scientific knowledge of fertilizers one would naturally think this would be a simple problem. It is possible to buy commercial fertilizer here but the high cost makes it unavailable for the average Indian landholder. Our neighbors agree that plowing under green manure crops such as legumes and lentils is a good idea. But the land they have now is not sufficient to raise food for the family for the entire year, how could they afford to plow under part of their crop? However, gradually, we hope to be able to encourage them to turn under green manure for soil improvement, even though it is only a small plot each year. Some farmers own sheep, goats, pigs and a team of oxen and by rotating their pen each year from field to field are able to improve their soil somewhat.

When our little school was first begun four years ago, a simple vegetable gardening class was introduced to help familiarize the children with a variety of vegetables totally lacking in the Indian diet. Each child has his own little plot and, besides, the children of the third and fourth grades are given plants and seeds to be planted at home in their own little garden plots. The agriculture teacher visits these gardens several times each year and makes suggestions as to how they can be improved. This has encouraged more vegetable gardening at home and as a result, the demand for lettuce and cabbage plants was almost greater than we could supply this past year. Since the school gardens supply many of the vegetables served in the noon lunch, the children are not only learning how to raise a variety of vegetables but are also learning to like to eat them.

With land reform in the 1960s and 1970s, some of the land that had been seized from the indigenous people was returned to them. Beyond Tia Maria's little house, down the road past Llano Grande, Mercedes points down a hillside toward the Valle de Tinallo, Tinallo Valley. "This land was always in my family," she says. "But a few years ago, a flower grower came and put a padlocked fence around it to make a greenhouse for growing flowers to export. I told him that it was not his land, but he said he could take it because it was not being used. When I tried to come here to plant corn, he threatened me with his dogs. I had to gather up documents to show that the land was always in my family. It took several trips to Quito to finally get him to move off the land. But I did it."

Enrique and Laura have been rich resources for understanding both past and present in Ecuador, and I thank them sincerely. We have a quick late lunch, and then Mercedes and I leave the house with our backpacks, water bottles, and hats to protect from the sun, heading for the Women's Cooperative Organic Garden. They're meeting today. "I got the idea of a cooperative garden from the backyard gardens I saw when I visited Virginia," Mercedes tells me.

At the entrance, there is a table set up to sell vegetables. We go through the gate, up the steps, and around the little house that serves as their headquarters. Rows of green vegetables stretch from one end of the enclosure to the other. Drip irrigation hoses lie along the rows. Women in light blue smocks with sun hats are busy hoeing. A pile of weeds is growing at the end of the garden.

The women leave their work and come over to be introduced and to talk. In addition to this garden, each woman also has a garden at home, and they vary the planting time so that they always have something to sell at their market stall. After talking a while in the garden, we gather on the porch behind the house and sit on benches for juice and *tostado* [parched corn]. They ask me questions about my life back home; they think maybe they could come for a visit. "We save up the profits from our sales for special trips. How much would a plane ticket to Indianapolis cost? Maybe we could save up enough so we can all go." They laugh.

We end with everyone telling their name and something about themselves. There is an easy camaraderie among those who had been with the group all of its eighteen years and the younger women. One young woman shares a recently experienced tragedy. "It was my turn to plant seeds. I had planted beets and celery. But my chickens got into the garden and ate all the seeds. Now I need to buy more seed and plant again."

Another woman with a scarred face and one cloudy eye recalls how Mercedes came to her at a particularly difficult time in her life and invited her to join the cooperative. "She saved my life, she did." Mercedes nods modestly. They proudly tell me they have never taken a bit of foreign aid for this project aside from the loan of an agronomist from a German foundation. As we leave, we buy some organic vegetables and a dressed chicken, which they put into their refrigerator for us since we had more walking to do.

Mercedes inherited land from her father. Her husband Andrés also inherited land from his family, both in Llano Grande and up the Guayllabamba Valley. Mercedes and Andrés have four children, and they have already divided their land among their children. But she fears that some of them may not keep the land. Their oldest son has a home in Quito. He works for a European NGO and his wife works for the Ministry of Education. Mercedes's youngest son is married to a Columbian refugee who grew up without the ties to land that my friends have.

"My husband's father and mother spent their whole lives building up their land in Ohio," I tell her. "But not one of their five sons was interested in farming the land. When his mother died a few years ago, the farm was sold. At least it was a cousin who bought it."

I know the situation is different. Yet, I think, as we leave behind these determined and productive women, there is something common about the ties to the land that people build when they have suffered and labored to make it their own.

It has been another great day, but I need to go to bed early tonight. My quiet life at home doesn't compare to the pace Mercedes has set for me here.

Chapter 20
La Comuna

I awake refreshed, and as I open a window of my bedroom in Elizabeth's house, I'm conscious of the freshness of the atmosphere in this place in the Andes. I leave tomorrow. We have walked many paths here, sharing our childhood memories and the destinations to which life has taken us in the many years since we were young ones together in this town.

When we were children, Mercedes often spent time in our home just as Jan and I spent time in her home. After church one Sunday during summer vacation, we begged Mom to let Mercedes spend the night with us. Together, we skipped through the woods between the school and the farm. The footpath required us to walk single-file around chunks of hard congahua and nettle shrubs whose little seeds clung to our socks; we jumped across a little ditch that could carry a torrent of water when it rained. Just before getting to the farm, the path descended down the side of the Quebrada Chica, the little ravine that ran from the road down to the Quebrada Grande, or big ravine. Coming out on the road, we climbed the short cobblestone drive up to the farm.

After our usual special lunch of fried chicken, mashed potatoes, and fresh peas, Mercedes walked around the table to where my mother was sitting and formally thanked her for the meal. "Why can't you kids be as polite as the little Ecuadorian children?" my mother wondered. Mercedes was two years older than I, and sometimes she seemed so mature and adult-like, wise beyond her years.

We spent the rest of the afternoon playing in the woods. There were little caves along the edges of the quebrada to visit. The mounds of ribbon grass offered ideal hideouts if we didn't mind getting scratched by the razor sharp leaves, and we followed trails left by rain runoff and made new trails ourselves. At the ends of those trails, we imagined that we might find a hidden cave full of Inca gold. In our childish ignorance, we even played cowboys and Indians, blissfully unaware of how that could have felt to Mercedes.

Tired and dusty, we arrived home ready for popcorn, homemade candy, and stories. As we started to get ready for bed, we realized that Mercedes had not brought pajamas. Mom suggested that she could sleep in her slip. "I'd rather sleep in pajamas," she said, so we loaned her a pair of yellow jersey PJs. Before getting into bed, Mercedes insisted on washing her feet because she did not wear shoes. After a lot of bouncing on the bed, we finally fell asleep on Mom and Dad's big double bed.

On another Sunday, Mercedes invited Jan and me home to her house for lunch. My parents commented that they had never had such an invitation. Children seemed to get into places where adults did not.

After church we walked to Mercedes's house at the far end of the village. Although buses could make it down that far, the road was really little more than a wide footpath. Cabuya and eucalyptus trees lined the road. Señor Pedro, Mercedes's father, led the way in his red striped poncho, his leathery brown face shaded by a brown felt hat, a Bible under his arm. Pedro, whom we all came to know as the village harpist and also as the church leader who became the discouraged outcast, was only present as Mercedes's dad that day. Her mom, Tia Maria, followed in her brightly embroidered blouse and red and gold beads. Earrings made of silver coins pierced her earlobes, and two shawls, one white with thin blue stripes and the second a heavier wool shawl, covered her head. Mercedes's outfit matched her mother's exactly. She tells me that her father always liked to see them dressed alike. Her two younger brothers, Enrique and Raul, ran ahead, hiding behind cabuya plants and jumping out to scare us. As they hid, they whistled wild bird songs to communicate with each other.

At the end of the road, we climbed up the bank and slipped through an opening in the hedgerow. Their house consisted of two rooms, joined by a covered porch, with one room used for sleeping. The other room was the kitchen. Over a fire in the middle of the kitchen, a clay pot of soup simmered, as guinea pigs scampered under the mud benches along the walls. The guinea pigs lived on the potato peels and other food scraps that fell to the floor during meal preparation. The roof of the house was thatched, allowing the smoke from the fire to filter up through the thatch. Their house was larger than most of the homes in the community, which only had one room, and they were also the only ones to use sleeping platforms, something Señor Pedro had seen in his travels to the coast.

Outside the house was a big adobe oven. When Señor Pedro heated up the oven to bake bread, neighbors also brought their dough to bake. On *Finados*, the Day of the Dead, it was, and still is, traditional to make *guaguas de pan*, bread dolls, and *colada morada*, a thick, deep purple corn and blackberry beverage, to eat at the graves of loved ones. The oven was always busy at that time of year.

Tia Maria pulled three stumps up to the little table set on the porch and served us soup made of mote and bits of pork. While we ate the soup from large soupspoons and dipped pieces of bread in the broth, Mercedes's parents and brothers sat along the wall on the mud benches to eat. I tried to remember to thank Tia Maria for the meal as I remembered Mercedes doing at our house.

After lunch, we ran out into the cornfield, hiding among the rows. The corn was still tender, so we looked for a stalk that did not have any ears. Enrique pulled a small knife from his pocket and cut the stalk into pieces for each of us, and with our teeth, we peeled back the fibrous outside and sucked the juice from the pulp, spitting the pulp onto the ground.

As the sun began to set behind the mountains, we sat on their porch, talking. Then, we saw the headlights of the approaching truck coming up the narrow road, and we knew that our day of visiting was over. Mom and Dad had come to pick us up and take us home to our beds.

Mercedes gets quiet as we sit together outside her daughter's house, recalling our childhood times together. "I have something to confess. It has troubled me all these years," she says. "When I slept over at your house, I stole a handkerchief from your mother. I know now that she would have gladly given it to me, if I had asked. But it was so pretty that I just took it."

I don't think my mother even missed the handkerchief. At least, she never mentioned it to me. I nod and feel my cheeks redden with my own shame from that same time. I think back to our games in the woods. "I confess that I called you '*India*, Indian.' You were the one who taught me that the name was demeaning and that I should refer to you and your people as '*Indigena*, Indigenous.' I learned something from you that day that still influences my efforts to undo racism in my own community."

Mercedes laughs lightly. "Ah, yes. Indigena. Now we prefer to be called Kitu Kara. We are part of the Kitu Kara Nation who resisted Inca domination before the Spanish came and dominated us. Our struggle to resist domination still goes on. It is a high purpose in our *comuna*."

"Help me understand the meaning of comuna," I ask Mercedes. I sense that it goes beyond community or even commune.

"Llano Grande just celebrated sixty-nine years of being a comuna," she says. "Before, we were just a scattering of families, spread across a wide area. When a comuna forms, a leader is chosen by consensus. It has to be someone of good character—someone who does not get drunk, who is faithful to his wife. This person is so highly respected that, when he calls the people, they come. He calls the people to mingas when there is a job to be done. When someone in the comuna is in need, the others gather around them to help." She makes a wide circle with her hands. "We care for each other. It isn't like the outside world, where it is each one for himself." I know that the definition includes also communally held resources such as pastureland and water.

We get up and move about the community one final time to see some specific changes time and the village's progressive movements have brought. Mercedes reminds me of places where she has led her neighbors in combating encroachment from the neighboring white communities. There is the fence that was erected by a businessman from Quito who planned to build a flower greenhouse on her family property. She has already told me how she had to confront the fence, the dogs, and his loaded gun with documents and sheer determination to keep him from going ahead with his plans. And there is the highway leading to the Quebrada Grande, built by the city of Quito to carry trash to the landfill they had planned in the Quebrada. Mercedes tells me about contacting an indigenous environmental engineer who documented the health risks of dumping garbage into the water source serving the whole area. With this information, she was able to get the neighboring white town of Calderon to join the indigenous people of Llano Grande in resisting the garbage dump that would have been detrimental to all of the people in the area. It took the joint effort to break down the long-term animosity and suspicion between the two communities. Getting the people of Calderon and Llano Grande to work together for a common goal was no small feat. The history of hostilities has been long and painful.

It is now afternoon. Andrés comes to Elizabeth's house with a gunnysack of freshly picked peas and some nugget candy, my favorite, made with the honey from his bees. I have not seen a lot of him this week, as he has been working on his land in Guayllabamba. As we sit at the table in the cool of the late afternoon, shelling peas, I ask about that painful time when he and others struggled to organize a decent transportation system. I have only vague images of it, things I heard from my parents in 1972, early in my own years of marriage.

"It was a difficult time in the 1970s," he says. "The Llano Grande bus cooperative we had organized in the past was going bankrupt. All we had been able to afford were old, wooden buses. They were unreliable, and two had burned up."

"That was when your mother and little sister were killed?"

"Yes, it was. One of our objectives was to have metal buses to avoid similar disasters. The bus service from Calderon was abusive. The drivers called us names and sometimes wouldn't even stop for a waiting passenger."

Mercedes comes out of the kitchen and joins us. In spite of what I now realize is their often difficult marriage, they continue to work together in their home and on their land and, together, they share this moving history with me. "There was a crippled old man who rode the bus into Quito to work as a street sweeper," she says. "One day, when he was not fast enough getting off the bus, the conductor shoved him off. He fell and hit his head on the cobblestones and died. When I saw that, I gathered the young adults at the church for a meeting."

Andrés continues. "La comuna, the community, decided to boycott the Calderon buses and to block the road into Llano Grande. Trenches were dug across the two roads leading into the community, and large eucalyptus trees were dropped across the road. Two groups of people took responsibility to wait at the blockade to prevent others from opening the roads. Without the buses going through the community to pick up people who needed to go into Quito to work or take their things to market, the people began to walk."

Mercedes describes the scene. "Every morning, lines of people, some carrying heavy loads, walked out to the Pan-American Highway to catch any available bus into Quito. And in the evening, they would all come walking back."

I can't help but think about the bus boycotts that were taking place in the U.S. at about the same time. I smile, not wanting to interrupt their story. We gather the peapods into a pile for the guinea pigs, which now live in a shed behind the house.

"Finally, a group of five hundred Llano Grande people went into Quito and walked the length of the city with a loudspeaker and placards to inform the general populace of our struggle and need for justice," Andrés says. "We went to the offices of the National Traffic Council and requested permission to have more buses for the Llano Grande cooperative. But we were met with threats to take away our permission to transport people to Quito at all, if we did not let the Calderon buses, owned by whites, move freely into our community."

Mercedes eagerly adds, "A second march was organized for a few days later. We made placards to tell our story. We all dressed in our native clothes, the men in their white pants and striped ponchos, the women in their embroidered blouses and anakos. Even more of us marched to Independence Plaza in front of the presidential palace and sat quietly on the steps of the National Cathedral, under the windows of the president."

"By coincidence," Andrés continues, "it was our good fortune that at that hour the president was receiving the ambassador of

Czechoslovakia or Russia. President Velasco Ibarra asked who was out there and what we wanted. While eight hundred of our people waited outside, five of us went up to meet with the president, including Mercedes's brothers Enrique and Raul, who was president of the cooperative, and me. Everyone was surprised at how educated and articulate these 'Indios' were, and they listened to our request for cooperation from the police in our efforts to provide bus service to the community."

"The white people of Calderon were furious that the 'Indios' had won," Mercedes says. "There was one white from Calderon who joined our cooperative. Other members wanted the cooperative to be only indigenous, but Raul, who was president of the cooperative, said, 'He is a good person. We should be more diverse. And, anyway, I went to school with him. He is very respectful.'

"But, then the guy said, 'I am a *Señor*. No Indian is going to tell me what to do.' We should have known that he would not be true to the cause. One night, this white guy was driving the bus, making the rounds at three in the morning. The people had picked ears of corn, pumpkins, and squash to take to the city to sell. So, at three in the morning, this woman got on the bus at Cuatro Esquinas, and she overhead the driver and the conductor talking. They said, 'Look, you get off and call Raul. Tell him we need to talk. When he comes, we will take him to the Two Bridges and throw him off.' Do you remember the Two Bridges?"

I shake my head "no" as we pour the shelled peas into a bowl and dip more pods from the gunnysack. Ernesto comes to the table to greet his grandparents on his way out to play in his treehouse. Mercedes pauses for him to leave the room before continuing. It is a painful story to recall. "It was at the end of Llano Grande, over the Quebrada Grande where no one lives, no one. When they got to my house, the conductor got off to call my brother. But, it turns out that Raul had already left with a loudspeaker to give news to the community. So he was not home. That was when they decided that Raul had to be eliminated."

"The next evening," Andrés continues, "he and I were walking home from a meeting. As we passed the chicharia at Cuatro Esquinas, the white guy's six brothers jumped out from behind the building. We tried to get away, but their sister came out and hit Raul behind the knees with a stalk of sugar cane, causing him to fall down. I had made it into the cornfield when I heard the bus start up. I heard a sound like a pumpkin being smashed and knew that they had run over Raul. It was his chest being crushed. They backed up and ran over him again. I had to go home and tell Mercedes that her younger brother had been killed."

I gasp. I had heard parts of the story, but it is even more shocking hearing it from Raul's family. It is hard to take in the pain of their loss even after all these years. Mercedes has told me that Raul was engaged to a young teacher when he died, compounding their grief. Mercedes nods. "When the comuna saw that we were not going to take vengeance, they were furious, so furious that they did not want to listen. So my mother, my father, my brother Enrique and I, we said 'No, that is not the way. We trust the authorities. Taking vengeance is not what Jesus taught.' "Meanwhile, the woman who had hit Raul with the sugar cane went around the community with a dagger, telling the people, 'See this dagger. If you testify for that Indio, we will split you like this. You saw what we did to that Indio. Think what we will do with you."

Andrés continues. "When we tried to get justice, the people who murdered Raul hired white 'witnesses' from other towns who lied and said that Raul was drunk and fell down. When Mercedes met them on the street, they would swear and say, 'No Indian is going to tell me what to do. You will not get the best of us.'" It has been forty-two years since this happened, but the pain and loss are still fresh. The tragedy seems to define the identity of this family.

Mercedes and Enrique had told me earlier that they avoided doing any business in the white town of Calderon for many years. They only came together with the people from Calderon when their mutual water supply was threatened. "Raul was the real, effective leader of the group," Andrés says. "He had real leadership potential, and that was lost with his murder. I am grateful for the church's teaching of pacifism. There have been times I was tempted to fight back but realized that it would not have made things better."

Buses from the Llano Grande cooperative now run back and forth between Quito and Llano Grande. The fleet now has many modern buses, purchased with money sent from Spain by the next generation of Kita Kara, who went to Spain to work as cooks, gardeners, and housekeepers. We take one of those buses into Calderon for me to buy some last-minute souvenirs. I comment that it now seems possible to get anywhere in Ecuador by bus. My city in the States lacks such extensive public transportation. Where I live, it is essential to have a car in order to get anywhere.

Mercedes looks puzzled. "Why doesn't your comuna get together, form a cooperative and buy a bus? Then people would not need to drive their cars." I smile at the thought of such a thing in my suburban neighborhood.

I am also smiling in anticipation. Tonight will be my farewell party, for goodbyes to old and new friends.

Chapter 21
Dios os guarde

Dios os guarde en su santo amor,
Hasta el día en que lleguemos,
A la patria do estaremos,
Para siempre con el Salvador.

Al venir Jesús nos veremos,
A los pies de nuestro Salvador;
Reunidos todos seremos,
Un redil con nuestro buen Pastor.

May God keep you in his holy love,
Until the day that we arrive,
In the land where we will be
Forever with our Savior.

When Jesus comes, we will meet again,
At the feet of our Savior;
Reunited we will all be,
In the fold of our good Shepherd.

I could never sing that song through without choking on the words. We always sang it in our church community when someone was leaving the country. It was loaded with the pain and grief of separation from people who had become such a significant part of our lives. I hated the song because it meant I had to say goodbye.

The little congregation would gather in the courtyard of the school, in front of the chapel steps. If a new missionary was arriving or a family was returning, we would crowd together and sing, "¡Bienvenidos! ¡Bienvenidos! Los hermanos hoy aquí nos gozamos en decir: ¡Bienvenidos! ¡Bienvenidos!" "Welcome! Welcome! The brethren here today are delighted to say: Welcome! Welcome!" Across the road that led into Llano Grande, a welcome gate was built with eucalyptus trunks and decorated with flowers. People gathered to meet the newcomers and guide them to the school, where a welcome feast had been prepared. We would clap and wave. The community shared in the joy and anticipation.

But, when someone was leaving, the feeling was completely different. We would meet in the little chapel to hear a beloved missionary preach his last sermon in that church. People would get up and share their love for the family who was leaving. Gifts were given, a small wood carving or a shawl from the new textile shop. Then we would gather in the courtyard. The little congregation was swollen by other people from the community who had also come to say goodbye. Some of the church women had been busy in the kitchen. The crowd gathered around a feast of boiled potatoes with hot peanut sauce, corn on the cob, and, my favorite, come y bebe, those barrels of fruit juice with pieces of fruit floating in them. I could almost let myself freely celebrate the festivities. But, I knew that it would end with that song.

In English, the first line of the song says, "God be with you 'till we meet again." Why did we have to sing about meeting these dear friends in heaven? I never wanted to wait that long to return to my beloved Ecuador. In 1959, on the day we at last left Ecuador, I looked around the courtyard with its hard-packed dirt surface. I remembered the schoolchildren gathered around their first Christmas tree, singing and laughing as they opened their gifts of combs, toothbrushes, and soap. I remember them lined up at the start of every school day singing the national anthem before going into their classes. The school had been painted, the walls built, the courtyard cleared during the mingas that had also concluded with the sweet come y bebe.

I looked around at my friends, especially Mercedes and her two brothers, Enrique and Raul. Mercedes had prayed at my baptism as I came up out of the water. There was Maria, who had cared for us while Mom worked at the school. When we'd left on furlough several years ago, Bobby had clung to her, crying "Ma-ri-aaa. Ma-ri-aaa." There was Segundo, who was always ready to play with us. On one New Year's Eve, he had helped us make a paper effigy of the old year to burn. There is my friend and playmate Andrés, who would eventually marry my friend Mercedes. And there were so many others. The women clad in brightly hand-embroidered blouses and anakos, shawls resting on their heads; the men in white shirts and pants with red or black striped ponchos. The bare feet that stood in the hard-packed dirt of the courtyard were cracked from walking through the fields and up and down the trails of the village. This was the community where I felt I belonged.

When it was finally time for my family to leave, after my father gave his last sermon, we crowded together in the courtyard and sang "Dios os guarde…" as best we could. Tears, sobs, choking on the words. Was it really true that we would only meet again at the feet of Jesus? To a fourteen-year-old, that felt like never.

I tried to keep in touch by mail, but the urgency of learning to fit into teenage life in the United States soon crowded out my efforts to keep in touch with a past that seemed so disconnected from where I now found myself. I had become a third culture kid and felt that I needed to leave my childhood in Ecuador behind. I would study nursing, volunteer in Brazil, marry, and raise four children. I would bury my mother and father, my husband, and one son.

In *You Can't Go Home Again*, Thomas Wolfe wrote about his main character (really about himself), "Why had he always felt so strongly the magnetic pull of home…? He did not know. All that he knew was that the years flow by like water, and one day men come home again."

After fifty-five years of being gone, I have come to the village where I grew up, where my family lived and cared for each other and the community. On my last night, as I prepare to say goodbye, we do not sing that song. Instead, we gather in the backyard for a wiener roast in a firepit behind Jorge's house. Mercedes, her husband Andrés, and their children, German, Elizabeth, Jorge, and Esthela, their husbands and wives and all of the grandchildren are there. So are Alfredo and his wife. Alfredo is the younger brother of Andrés, the boy who came to stay with them when his mother died. He has had so much bitterness toward the church for not intervening when his father was beating his mother. But he recently has been in remission from cancer and is so thankful that he gave the church a new roof in thanksgiving. The heritage of Christian presence and caring seems to live on in this family.

Mercedes tells them about spending the night at our house when we were children. Her daughters exchange glances and giggle. "You probably gave them lice, *Madre*."

While we talk, the younger children have fun playing hide-and-seek in the dark. How well I remember playing hide-and-seek outside after dusk. There is even a big stand of rhubarb to hide in, just like we used to have in the garden behind the house on the hacienda.

German gets out his guitar, and we sing. Some of the songs I remember and some I don't. Then come the speeches. Elizabeth talks about how much my visit has meant to her mother at this time when she is feeling the weight of aging and the responsibilities for her children. Jorge, born after the last missionaries left Llano Grande, tells how he has heard about the work of the missionaries and how much different Llano Grande is now. Again, I hear how much it meant to the people that Dad came back a few years ago, just prior to his death, and begged the community's forgiveness for his assumptions when he came as a young missionary. Esthela says how much it meant to her that I held her baby Hugito, talked with him, and gave him his bottle.

At the end of the other speeches, I talk about coming in search of a part of myself that I left behind fifty-five years ago and finding a place in this loving family. And we end by holding hands in a circle and praying.

Perhaps I have finally come home.

Benton Rhoades in later years with Enrique Tasiguano and his granddaughter, Barbara. Benton returned to Ecuador to visit old friends and process the changes in the region and in his own beliefs.

Pedro's Family, (l–r) Raul, Enrique, Mercedes, Tia Maria, and Pedro Tasiguano. How young these parents look! And they were young in these days when Mercedes was our good friend.

The harpist Pedro Tasiguano.

Mount Pichincha overlooking modern Quito, captured by me on a recent trip.

Mercedes and Jeanne in recent days.